DEVELOPMENT WITHOUT AID

Development Without Aid

The Translucent Society

by

LEOPOLD KOHR

Foreword by
Kenneth D. Kaunda
President of Zambia

Critical Reflections by
Professors Robert J. Alexander
and Alfred P. Thorne

Christopher Davies Wales

TO

DONNA 'TIFFANY' PACE

SBN 7154 0044 4

First published in 1973
by Christopher Davies (Publishers) Ltd.,
Llandybie, Carmarthenshire
Printed by
The Merlin Press,
Llandybie, Carmarthenshire

TABLE OF CONTENTS

FOREWORD

NYONE concerned with the problems of making decisions about economic development is confronted with a quite bewildering array of choices. Very often the developed nations are held up as models; some of them are capitalist, some have semi-socialist welfare-state systems, and others are communist; yet even within each of these categories there are pronounced differences. Capitalist U.S.A. is a different proposition to capitalist Switzerland, welfare state socialist Sweden is of another order to the apparently similar British system, and communist Russia is using different approaches to communist China—and both are difficult to categorise with communist Yugoslavia.

All of these models can show some success and all of them seem to betray some drawbacks. What are the factors that account for their failures?

These questions, and many others, cannot be divorced from the practical problems of economic and social development today, for clearly, somewhere along the road a number of mistakes *have* been made and, if we fail to pinpoint them accurately, we shall run the risk of repeating them.

It is mainly this task of pinpointing them which Professor Kohr undertakes in this volume.

If I may anticipate some of his arguments in different words, it seems to me that economic theory has been dominated for too long by what may be called an excessive *quantum* approach. This may be very suitable for someone marooned on a desert island, or who may be starving from other causes; in such cases, clearly, quantity is all. But once this urgent concern for mere survival has been met then, surely, other factors come to the fore: factors which, whilst not displacing that of quantity, bring in considerations of size, of scale, and above all, of *quality*. It is this which seems to me to mark out the essential difference between the case put forward by Professor Kohr and those which he has generously invited and included in this volume, from Professor Alfred

i

Thorne and Professor Robert Alexander, as well as most orthodox opinion.

Man is not a consumption machine, nor are human societies,
if they are truly human, mere statistical aggregations. So that
when Professor Alexander urges that "foreign assistance has been
of very great aid in the furthering of the development of more
backward nations," he does not raise at all the problem of the
kind of society that aid has helped to promote or even determine,
and it is this problem which is now of paramount concern.

Paramount if only because the developed nations have apparently so sedulously ignored it in relation to themselves.

Even now, they are trying to ignore these considerations, and
yet when one appraises the multiple signs of stress, economic
uncertainty and the hitherto neglected evidence of ecological
disruption, the undermining of complex life-support systems in
nature, and the psychic deterioration of human beings, all apparently stemming largely from economic malpractice, their problems must give us all a prompting to reconsider where we are
going.

So much expert advice being given to under-developed countries today has the effect of helping to solve one aspect of the
problem under consideration whilst creating a number of others
which are worse than the original, and in our own experience in
Zambia not only has this frequently happened, but I am struck by
the number of occasions on which we have achieved excellent
results in defiance of expert advice which has been rendered!

In this volume Professor Kohr has succeeded in throwing a
flood of light on many problems which up till now underdeveloped countries have found intractable. In our Zambian par-
lance he may well be called the first Humanist Professor of
Economics, for his work is concerned with human societies rather
than such arid abstractions as "economic man" and his goal is
always not simply quantitative multiplication, important as that
may be, but what he himself repeatedly calls the *summum bonum*
—the good life.

But let no one think this is merely another dry addition to

what is called "the dismal science". Professor Kohr writes with a wit, a sparkle, a lucidity and an elegance which is seldom met in any technical writing. He is, moreover, not writing by rote as it were; one is conscious that he is bringing a continuous creative effort of the intellect to bear, and the ensuing excitement of his narrative is as rare as it is rewarding.

There may well be some unperceived pitfalls in seeking to apply Professor Kohr's model to actual life, but that is in the nature of things. What matters is that he has said something new, something important, something which no-one concerned with development problems can afford to ignore and something which I am sure everyone can read with both pleasure and profit.

> KENNETH D. KAUNDA
> President.

State House, Lusaka,
The Republic Of Zambia.
February, 1972.

ACKNOWLEDGEMENTS

Ridentem dicere verum, quid vetat ?
—HORACE

M Y gratitude is due to a number of friends for a variety of reasons. To Robert and Joan Alexander, William and Alice Bagley, Henry and Elsa Klumb, Anatol and Orlene Murad, Simon and Mabbie Schmiderer, Alfred and Vivi Thorne, for challenging my ideas with such unrelenting vigour; to the late Sir Herbert Read, for sharing so warmly a fellow anarchist's enthusiasm for the small; to Dr. E. F. Schumacher, for the inspiration I derived from the extraordinary parallelism of his ideas, reaching often into minute detail; to Mary Dassier and Peter Wenzel for their friendship; to Barrows Mussey and six distinguished editors: Alwyn Rees of the Welsh-language Monthly *Barn,* Alex Maldonado of *El Mundo,* William Dorvillier and Andrew Viglucci of *The Sun Juan Star,* John Papworth and Roger Franklin of *Resurgence,* for extending the hospitality of their pages to so many of my unorthodoxies; very specially to Donna 'Tiffany' Pace for her spirited editorial criticism; to Alun Talfan Davies, and to Alwyn Rees a second time, for their invaluable general assistance; and particularly also to my comrades in arms: Dr. Edgar Berman, Dr. Gerald Feigen, the late Howard Gossage, Scott Newhall, and Franc Ricciardi, for the magnanimity with which they let themselves be drawn into a campaign to apply the development theories of this book to the little Caribbean island state of Anguilla.

PREFACE

Nature suffers nothing to remain in
her kingdom that cannot help itself.
—EMERSON

THIS book is an extension of a series of lectures given at two Conferences: on *Nationalism,* at Oxford University in July 1963, and on *The Economics of Independence* at University College of Wales, Aberystwyth, in January 1969. It offers an alternative solution to the assisted sort of development which the leaders of underdeveloped countries seem to prefer in their effort to catch up with modern times as rapidly as possible. In contrast to what I have to propose, they feel that lavish help is the least their former masters should offer in redemption of their past sins, and the least to which the young nations are entitled for being held in colonial subjection and retardation for so long.

Morally, they may well be right. But politically and nationally, the result of assisted development is the opposite to what the newly liberated countries can desire. What does assisted development mean? It means the importation of an amplitude of cars, equipment, machinery, and designs from the countries supplying the assistance. But it also means that, with it, comes an army of consultants, advisers, engineers, architects showing how the equipment is to be used, the machinery set up, the designs executed.

This in turn leads to the importation of the spirit of the country that has invented all these things in response to its own needs and traditions, not theirs. As a result, the assisted country, which may have fought wars and revolutions for the right to determine its own national standards, soon finds itself alienated from itself by insensibly adopting the features of the very countries whose mentality it may consider incompatible with its own aspirations. And since the country most eagerly called upon to render assistance is the United States, the alienation following in the footsteps

9

of assisted development amounts actually to a process of Americanization.

This, of course, is not desired by modern nation builders either. So they choose as one way out of the dilemma the method of importing freely the aid and goods, while trying to keep out the spirit, of the assisting countries. Lowering their economic barriers against commodities, they feel compelled to raise at the same time their emotional barriers against the infiltration of the alien mind by fanning hatred and contempt for the very peoples sending them the commodities. Castigating them for their past, doubting their present intentions, and vilifying the low commercialism of their future design, they nevertheless grab up their Trojan gifthorse Cadillacs, hoping that continued abuse will get them a few more. Yet, however effective hatred may be as a group-builder, it cannot prevent the gradual erosion of the traditional native identity under the assimilating pressure of imported progress. For whoever begins to sip Coca Cola, and switches too rapidly from a mule to a car and television civilization, is eventually bound to become in habit and taste an American irrespective of whether his subtitles and instruction labels are written in Spanish or Singhalese.

And there is yet another danger to the ceaseless use of hatred and recrimination as an identity builder. It can be driven too far. For the assisters, however conscience-stricken they may once have been, may, like the historically uninvolved generation of post-Nazi Germans, some day decide that they have been castigated long enough; that those unable to stand on their economic feet *without* aid, may not be able to stand on them *with* aid either; that, in fact, they have been given the burden of freedom too soon and as a result must be placed under tutelage once more.

In other words, instead of waxing rich on conscience-money, the recently liberated countries may hate themselves into the second age of colonialism with the result that their leaders, already responsible for the destruction of their peoples' national identity through their stubborn insistence on importing assisted economic development from the outside, will also turn out to be the grave diggers of their countries' political independence. And all because the new breed of open-shirted, bearded, magnificently gowned, megalomaniacal palace-dwellers cannot resist the lure of a million bucks a day from the American Treasury.

Yet, as this book tries to show, there is an alternative open to post-colonial leaders that runs none of these dangers. This is to gain economic maturity *without* assistance; to foster, as the title page suggests, Development *Without* Aid.

This is, of course, considerably harder. But it is precisely the shared experience of hardship which has always proved to be by far the most reliable tool by which people have acquired the common features identifying them as members of the same group. Indeed, self-development is not merely an effective *alternative* way of nation building. Historically, as Marx would phrase it, it was the *primary* way. Every country that is today fully developed, economically grown up, and emotionally mature, has gained its status not by jumping in infantile contemporary fashion on the shoulders of somebody else's experience. Every one of them gained it by singlehandedly wresting it from forbidding hostile environments in personally suffered trial, error, blood and sweat and toil and tears.

Indeed, it would be difficult to find a single precedent in history of a nascent nation ever stooping to ask for help during the pain-filled process of becoming itself. What created the Greek, Roman, German, French, Spanish, Icelandic, American, Swedish, Russian, Japanese, Chinese national communities was invariably the internally shared experience of hardship, hardship, hardship, hardship. Suffering ruggedly, determinedly, and uncomplainingly, the face of every individual began in due course to reflect the lines of the common struggle, the imprint by which each recognized in the other membership in the same collective being. There was no need for strengthening the rising group consciousness through the xenophobic vilification of outsiders. Shared hardship had made it strong enough. And not only this. It was the hardship, deprivation and sacrifice of the period of their ascent which made it possible for the now developed nations to accumulate those much-maligned riches which enable them today to extend the doubtful blessing of their help to the still underdeveloped countries. But there is of course no reason why the latter should not be able to accumulate the same riches under their own steam. All they need to do is to duplicate what made their assisters so prosperous: forego the pleasures of alimony income and, instead, raise themselves by their bootstraps, however tough this may appear.

This should be the more appealing if one considers that, in contrast to the historic "bootstrap" method, the contemporary variety of assisted development is a paradoxical senility phenomenon--paradoxical because the nations soliciting help are not decrep¡tly tottering with age but claiming the full vigour of youth.

The only argument in favour of assisted development is that it might accelerate advance by sparing the rising nations the wasteful trouble of having to duplicate every painful experience of social growth on their own flesh. But, again, if children are spared the duplication of everything through which the parents had to go, they will not grow up faster but suffer even longer from dependence on those who *did* take the trouble of doing the experiencing and learning themselves. Moreover, just as the duplication of experience does not take a child more than two decades to catch up with everything discovered before its time, so does the process of duplicating independent growth, by which normally endowed young nations develop from economic infancy to maturity, not take more than a generation. It may take ages before the seed begins to sprout. But once it **has** taken roots, the period of germination which nature has provided is always of the briefest.

Hence, one may cite both history and national biology as witness to the fact that not only were all previous giant developmental leaps forward of the unassisted variety, but that the unassisted variety was invariably so rapid once it got afoot that even acceleration is no argument for soliciting aid. On the contrary. For while an unnaturally accelerated pace of assistance often does produce precocious offspring, it tends to distort the growth process itself to such an extent that the assistance that started it can never again be withdrawn. It becomes a budget item, and dependence a perpetual sore.

What this volume proposes is therefore nothing new. It is as old as time. All it suggests is to go back to the *natural* way of handling problems of growth. This may seem reactionary and too slow for the impatient angry young revolutionaries of our age.

And they may have a point there. It has taken nature in its unharassed and ever backward-looking ways a long nine months to develop us unaided from conception to birth. With the aid of the newest in revolutionary medical machinery it might have brought us forth in six—fragile, unviable, swollen-headed. But with what speed!

*"American plant, Russian equipment,
German assembly, Czech parts
—all the fruit of our
good old neutralist know-how."*

HOW TO LOSE NATIONAL IDENTITY THROUGH AID.

Reproduced by permission of PUNCH

Part 1

THE THEME

"The higher a thing is, the more self-sufficient it is; since whatever needs another's help is by that fact inferior. But that city is more fully self-sufficient which the surrounding country supplies with all its vital needs, than is another which must obtain these supplies by trade."

—THOMAS AQUINAS.

Chapter One

DEVELOPMENT BY COMMON MARKET

By the time a great power learns of a difficulty,
we in Liechtenstein are half way through solving it.

—DR. ALEXANDER FRICK

W HAT escapes many a modern nation builder striving for
more rapid development through the greater economic
integration of their states with their neighbours is that
by far the fastest way of developing is by going it alone—unintegrated, unaffiliated, unco-ordinated.

This is contrary to current dogma. Dazzled by the success of
the European Common Market, there is a consensus of opinion
that all that is needed for speedy progress is banding together.[1]
However, the secret of the Common Market's success lies not in
the union of its members but in the type of members that joined.
None of them has become prosperous only recently. Each has
·ranked as one of the world's foremost industrial nations for at
least a century. They joined the club not as paupers but as
millionaires. They united not *in order* to mature but *after* they
had matured; *after* their individual economies had become so

---

1 The strength of the banding-together philosophy can be measured by the
British effort to join a perfectly satisfied and flourishing Mauritius to a less
prosperous larger territory for no other reason than the orthodoxy of principle, which may make sense to statesmen but hardly to a Mauritian.
According to a report to *The Times* (London, November 6, 1961) from Port
Louis, Mr. J. Arbuthnot, Conservative M.P. for Dover, one of a team of
visiting British parliamentarians, "said that they had been impressed by what
they had seen of Mauritius life. They paid tribute to the working of the
Mauritius legislative Council, though they thought that *on grounds of
principle* there was a case for Mauritius to be linked with a wider federation
in the Commonwealth" (italics mine). What on earth is the principle for the
sake of which a flourishing separate community should be drowned in the
admittedly not so flourishing unity of greater multitudes? It is the same
principle that years later led to the famous Anguilla crisis.

strong that they could afford the luxury of a common superstructure. No wonder they flourish.

The opposite is true of underdeveloped countries such as for example the island states of the Caribbean. Here, the idea of union is advanced not as the fruit of prior development but as a means of achieving it. This makes about as much sense as ten-year-old children wanting to get married for the purpose of speeding up their maturing process, the bridegroom confidently informing the prospective father-in-law, anxiously inquiring whether he has the funds for the enterprise: "No, but you have." Obviously, instead of maturing the children, the joining in marital union would retard them, and perpetuate an infancy that would be the costlier the more adult the trimmings.

And the same applies to the infant societies of underdeveloped countries. Also in their case the condition most conducive to rapid growth is not the existence but the absence of burdensome premature partnerships, particularly if this is coupled with the smallness of their territorial size, which offers them the translucency of proportions without which no social problem can find its proper solution. Here lies their great advantage over the scale-afflicted vision-dimming dimensions which result when regions are incorporated in the obscuring frame of enlarged territorial entities *before* their economies have the chance to strengthen their locally conditioned separate foundations. For only after each region has been allowed to solidify in the context of its own environment, can a local economy safely be used as a supporting pillar for collective structures larger than its own.

Nothing could illustrate this proposition better than the examples of early Italian, German, French, Dutch, or Belgian economic growth. In no instance was this due to organized large-scale co-operation or mutual assistance at the national level. In each case, the tremendous wealth inherited by the subsequently unified nations resulted from the independent, unintegrated, competitive rival activities of a host of small sovereign local communities who would have rejected not only with indignation but with armed force the suggestion of joining hands with neighbours in the interest of faster development. 800 years ago Venice looked very much like Puerto Rico's lagune slum of El Fanguito, Siena like Buen Consejo, Padua like Loiza Aldea, Porto Fino like Fajardo

in contrast to such lagging giants as India or Pakistan, a small state such as Liechtenstein with a population of barely 17,000 could achieve a bootstrap development during the past 15 years second only to that of Iceland (population 170,000) or the more publicised similar achievement of Puerto Rico (population 2.5 million), it would be ridiculous to suggest that the same process could not be duplicated in Trinidad, Antigua, or Barbados.

However, before these ideally-sized communities can get anywhere, they must end sponsoring development studies that are costlier than action;[1] cease pleading with others to join them in common endeavour; and stop sitting around in the subdued relaxation of sumptuous cocktail lounges in air-conditioned resort hotels, wasting their time in soul-searching consultation with expense-account batteries of high-powered advisors hiding their absence of *action* in the bustle of well reported *activity*. Instead they must at last begin listening to the experience of past nation builders such as Philip von Hornick who, in a famous blueprint for early 17th century bootstrap programmes told an economically sorely retarded Austria that she can lift herself "above all others, if she only wills it"—without common markets or the need of borrowing a penny from anyone else.[2]

[1] The sum of a full million dollars was allocated in 1963 by the Puerto Rican Planning Board not for the solution but the mere study of the traffic problems of San Juan, a minor connurbation of half a million inhabitants. It goes without saying that a sum so vast can only be earned in work lasting so long that, it must of necessity describe conditions that will long have ceased to exist by the time the study is completed.

[2] Some underdeveloped regions are in fact becoming receptive to doctrines similar to Philip von Hornick's. Thus Eric Kierans, Minister of Revenues of Quebec, which is still underdeveloped in spite of her long association with the rest of rich Canada, is one of a growing number of influential persons who maintain that his province could achieve a more satisfactory and faster development, if it only wills it, by going it alone. "This is an immensely rich province," he declared, according to the New York Times of February 24, 1964, much of it still underdeveloped. With its geographical position athwart the St. Lawrence River, Quebec most certainly would survive as a viable state. Of course, we would have to face a lowering in the standard of living, at any rate at first. But there would be tremendous compensations, especially in the emotional sphere." As I am trying to show in the two following chapters, there would not even be a need for lowering her living standards provided Quebec would give meaning to separation by developing along patterns of her own rather than those set by the rest of Anglo-Saxon North America.

Or, they might follow the example of proud Prime Minister Frick of Liechtenstein who, when I put to him the hypothetical question whether he would appreciate aid from a rich country such as the United States, answered with a touch of indignation: "Look here: by the time a great power learns of a difficulty, we are half way through solving it."

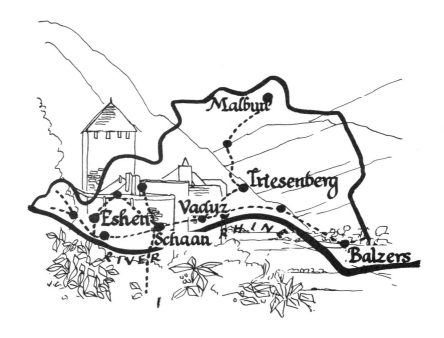

PRINCIPALITY OF LIECHTENSTEIN.
" IT CAN BE TAKEN IN AT A SINGLE VIEW."

Chapter Two

DRAWBACKS OF SELF-SUFFICIENCY

*Earth provides enough to satisfy every
man's need, but not every man's greed.*
—GHANDI

TRUE, the fruit of an inner-directed and largely isolated
and self-sufficient economic development resulting from
a succession of unassisted, unco-ordinated, competing
individual efforts would be radically different from the identity
destroying international standardization fostered by current planning. It would emphasize not electronic construction or steel
mills, the new objects of tribal worship, as Colin Clark has called
them, but a diversity of activities that are natural to the environment of each country. It would stress not the archaic mercantilist
idea of increasing trade which has lead to those unwholesome
lop-sided one-crop economies, but the socially infinitely more
beneficial target of increasing consumption which leads to diversification. It would enlarge the market not in width but in depth.
And by saving the tremendous waste of integration, communication, and transportation costs attached to the price of everything in far-flung international economies, it would make possible
the rapid achievement of a high standard of living at low cost
rather than the slow achievement of a not so high standard of
living at high cost, as is inevitable when development is geared
to transport-devouring large-scale integration right from the
beginning.

Even the United States could never have developed so fast
had not the country's economy in its early development stages
been split into countless uncostly isolated local pioneer societies
advancing separately rather than in unison. Thomas Balogh, the
eminent Oxford economist, has well expressed the developmental
unwisdom of unification when he warned a Britain anxious to

join the Common Market against the pitfall of such a union.[1] The economy of Scotland, he stressed, was thrown back by at least 150 years as a result of her union with England; of Ireland by 200; Wales has not overcome the shock yet. It took Hungary until 1923 to overcome the retarding effect of her leap backward into economic union with Austria in 1867. And Calabria, long united with Italy, and Brittany long united with France, are underdeveloped to this day.[2] Yet Thomas Balogh, though now a Lord, is supposed to be an economist not of the reactionary insular right but of the progressive internationalist left.

The principal "drawback" of self-sufficient localism is that it must forego a lot of status-conferring high-cost international amenities. In many places houses could not be built in concrete or supplied with plumbing imported from Chicago. But what is wrong with native stone or wood? Is there anything more beautiful and lasting than the stone houses built 500 years ago by medieval peasants in the Cotswolds, or the mountain houses built of sturdy wood in the storm-lashed altitudes of Switzerland? And what about plumbing, this high-priced symbol of modern living standards? There was excellent stone and marble plumbing

[1] Thomas Balogh, in a lecture before the Marshall Society of Cambridge University, attended by the author in winter 1961. Having ascribed the economic retardation of Scotland, Ireland, Wales, etc., to their union with England, the otherwise radical Lord Balogh has not yet become so radical as to suggest, in logical extension of his argument, curing their retardation by cutting them away from a United Kingdom which, according to his own testimony, was such an obstacle to their development.

[2] Gunnar Myrdal has, in his *Rich Lands and Poor* (New York: Harper & Brothers, 1957), created a special "theory of circular and cumulative causation," in order to explain the economic retarding effect of common markets between less and more advanced regions. Singling out the Italian and American examples, he writes: "The hampering of industrial growth in the poorer southern provinces of Italy, caused by the pulling down of internal walls after Italy's political unification in the 19th century, is a case in point which has been thoroughly studied: industry in the northern provinces had such a lead and was so much stronger that it dominated the new national market, which was the result of political unification, and suppressed industrial efforts in the southern provinces. . . . Another example is the long stagnation after the Civil War up till the Second World War of the Southern United States. As I shall argue . . ., this systematic bias of trade as between regions forms also part of the mechanism of exploitation in the economic relations between a metropolitan country and its colonies."

in self-sufficient Mycenae 3,000 years ago, and I myself only a few summers ago built in a day's much enjoyed labour a drainage system out of hollowed wood gathered from the grounds which looks better to me than the expert-estimated $200.00 alternative in modern piping which would have required a fund raising journey to an international assistance association.

Another "drawback" would be that our dinner table would lack the infinite variety of an international cuisine. No caviar from Russia! No smoked cheese from Austria! No ham from Poland! No gin from Holland! No beer from Bavaria! But how infinite *is* our absorptive capacity? The items of a local menu of a largely self-sufficient Austrian country inn, as a statistician friend has worked out for me, could be presented in more than 200,000 different combinations before having to bow to the monotony of repetition.

And what is wrong with the unsophisticated simplicity of a native table? It will be cheaper.[1] But will a Sicilian therefore consider spaghetti with mussels, tomato sauce and local wine a meal for serfs rather than a feast for the gods? Will Burgundians, as a cartoon once pictured, envy the affluence of American tourists who, when offered in a local café a bottle of home grown wine, replied, "We don't want that domestic stuff! We want imported stuff!" Does a Norman consider his a low standard of living because his inexpensive local cuisine can offer him no more than Rouen duck, hare, salt-marsh mutton, Norman sole, lobster, shrimp, oysters, pork sausage (*andouille*), Tournedos

---

1 Since my radical friends suspect my praise of unsophisticated culinary simplicity as a reactionary desire to maintain primitive levels for the primitive, let me quote from a review of the radical *New Statesman* (July 12, 1963) of a book on *Greek Cookery* by Joyce Stubbs: "I have eaten many memorable dishes prepared by Mrs. Stubbs . . . both in Athens and in her island hideout where the most primitive materials emerge from the brushwood oven with true distinction. Here, I think, is the clue to the best of Greek cooking—it is based on the simplest possible ingredients. Fish—often of species which English salt-and-water cooks consider too coarse for the table—olives, rice, birds, herbs and honey. . . . This, in other words, is a peasant cuisine; and though it has been developed by a few artists to a high international standard, the best Greek dishes are still the thrifty ones. There is no reason except unfamiliarity why most of them should not be prepared as successfully—and as economically—in Britain as in Greece."

steak, buttered carrots, string beans, Camembert and Pont-L'Evéque cheese, mussels in cream, cream-topped baked apples, pear and plum tarts, artichokes in vinegar and oil, salad greens, Calvados brandy, and vin ordinaire? This is why a place such as the faculty club of the University of Puerto Rico, when it recently decided to stress once again the offerings of the land rather than of the world, justly thought it was thereby not lowering but raising the standards of its cuisine.

Thus, if our modern nation builders are able to free themselves of their common-market fixation, they may yet come to realize that, while 100% of man's *summum bonum* can be achieved very expensively through international integration and co-operation, provided all of the co-operating parties are rich enough to afford it, the same 100% can also be achieved quite cheaply by concentrating on self-sufficient, unaffiliated, local development in the manner of the city-states of the Renaissance. It conveys a different *summum bonum*, but *summum bonum* nonetheless. And it has the added advantage that underdeveloped countries in search of dignity, identity, and independence can all finance it themselves. As Marx would have put it, all they must do is to give proper direction to the tremendous forces dormant not in the American Treasury but in the lap of social labour of every community, even if it be as small as a monastery.

But few nation builders can attempt this historically well tested and uncostly alternative road of rapid development as long as their advisors continue to build model upon model depicting for regions in Africa, Latin America, or the Caribbean a neatly synchronized, standardized, disindividualized, interlaced future in which every island state has been assigned to play a complementary cog-wheel role within the larger context of a common market.

The first step must therefore be to encourage the detailed elaboration of models picturing the opposite of the current fashion, that is to project the cost, quality, level, and looks of a development achievable in each underdeveloped region through a maximum degree of self-sufficiency and a minimum of time-wasting interdependent fraternization and work-preventing hand-holding. The establishment of ultimately desired bonds can then be left to the natural course of events spontaneously setting in at the end of the maturing process, rather than to the visionary romanticism of central planners sailing under the diagrammatic flag of mathe-maticized irrationality.

"Of course, they didn't have radio or television or anything in those days, and I suppose they had to do something."

Drawing by Stan Hunt. ©1959
The New Yorker Magazine, Inc.

Chapter Three

UNITED STATES, SOVIET UNION, AND LOIZA ALDEA

The man who small things scorns will next
By things still smaller be perplexed.

—GOETHE

EVERY now and again one reads comparisons between the respective costs in terms of labour-time of goods produced in the Soviet Union and the United States. They always make fascinating reading. And they are usually consoling. The Soviet economy may have produced the first sputnik. But it still takes a Russian worker the wages of 15 years to buy a house, while his American counterpart needs only those of 5. Hence, as far as housing is concerned, the American living standard is considered three times higher than the Russian. And there is nothing wrong with this computation. Yet, as is so often the case when figures are involved, it is misleading. It gives a correct picture, but not a complete one.

To gain a more complete picture, I have often been tempted to work out the comparative costs for a series of basic living standard items involving a slightly enlarged set of at least three regions: the Soviet Union, the United States, and a paradisiacal primitive village such as Loiza Aldea on the north coast of Puerto Rico, or any similar village you might think of in Bali, Ecuador, or Anguilla. Having not done so yet, I am lacking exact figures. Perhaps a sumptuous Ford grant can correct the situation. But, in the meantime, I feel confident that my findings would show approximately the following:

If it takes 15 years to acquire a unit of dwelling in the Soviet Union, and 5 in the United States, the cost in Loiza Aldea is probably in the neighbourhood of 2 weeks. Thus, if the American housing standard is 3 times higher than the Russian, the stand-

Harbour, beautiful even in its misery. And similar examples could be cited in every country, from Chile to Catalonia and England. Had they waited for Italy to be united, the Common Market to be formed, the Alliance for Progress to be launched or for Harvard and MIT missionaries to supersede the local genius, they would look in all likelihood by now like England's council-house communities, Salzburg's Maxglan, the San Juan sub-urbanization that goes by the name of Country Club, or the park Puerto Rico's Planning Board wants to put in the place of what should be another Amalfi or Positano—La Perla, the breathtaking back drop of Oscar Lewis' *La Vida*.

Managing their development without reliance on others, the luminous Italian city states not only produced a wealth in aesthetic and material splendour such as no present generation can afford with all its steel mills and standardized interchangeable mass production, and all the international co-operation and aid agencies put together. By exploiting to the utmost their local resources in stone, or wood, or clay, or marble, they insured to each a personality and identity of such sparkling difference that their face can still be recognized in spite of the contemporary tide of an otherwise indistinguishable and undistinguished universal brotherhood of man to whose protagonists, preaching union irrespective of race, colour, creed, or sex, a justly disgusted Frenchman has referred as *çes gens sans race, sans couleur, sans sexe*.[1]

Now I do not know such little states as Barbados, Antigua, or Trinidad. But one thing I feel certain about is this: If medieval Lucca with a population of less than 20,000 could achieve so splendid a development in so short a creative spurt not in co-operation but in competition with an equally splendid Pisa barely ten miles away (and because of going it alone, has to this day been able to retain its identity in spite of the internationalizing effect of modern tourism and industrialization); and if, in our own time,

---

[1] Both the surviving sparkling differences and the unrivalled riches of local in contrast to national development is well expressed by an advertisement of the Italian State Tourist Office, showing a glittering palace on Venice's Canale Grande, and proudly captioning it, "NO THIS IS NOT 'ITALY'. In Italy the houses are stone . . . here they are lace! In Italy the sun shines brightly . . . here it shimmers among shadows! For Venice is a 'state' all its own—in its culture, its climate, its Arabian Nights architecture."

ard of Loiza Aldea is 140 times higher than the American, and 420 times higher than the Russian. Similarly, if it takes a Russian the sacrifice of 20 minutes of labour time to acquire a unit of food (a loaf of bread for example), and an American 5 minutes, it may take the man from Loiza Aldea 10 seconds. All he has to do is to give the hammock on his porch in which he rests in air-conditioned comfort a gentle swing, and snatch a delicious unit of banana from the bush outside his door. So if the basic American food standard is 4 times higher than that of the Soviet Union, that of Loiza Aldea is 30 times higher than the American. And if it takes a Russian the sacrifice of 2 weeks of labour to acquire a shirt,[1] and an American half a day, it takes no time at all for the native of Loiza Aldea. For the happy man, living in the gentle breeze of shady coconut groves near his surf-sprayed sunny beach, does not wear a shirt. So again, if the American shirt standard is 28 times higher than the Russian, in Loiza Aldea it is infinitely higher than both, and healthier at that.

Now, one will say that this second extended comparison of living standards is even more misleading than the first. For a thatched-roofed bamboo hut, however romantic, cannot be put on the same footing as a bathroom-equipped stone house. A shirtless or, at least, a Bikini standard of undress, however comfortable, cannot be compared with the dress standard represented by Savile Row or Christian Dior. And a banana, however delicious, is not a vitamin enriched loaf of bread. In other words, while the cost of life may be cheaper in Loiza Aldea, the standard of life must still be considered infinitely higher in both America and Russia.

However, this is precisely what does *not* necessarily follow. When an Italian, savouring a plate of spaghetti and a bottle of wine, was told that the British standard of living was five times higher than his, he was not at all impressed. On the contrary!

[1] Those who envision paradise as an affluent welfare state, will undoubtedly consider the idea of a shirtless Loiza Aldea as reactionary romanticism. Yet the author of the charming fable of the Shirt of the Happy Man is no less a radical than Tolstoy. As his story goes, when a sufferer is told that he will regain his health if he wears the shirt of a happy man, he sets out on a vain search high and low. No one is happy. In the end he comes to a beggar who is the first to admit that he is. But when the sufferer asks for his shirt, the happy beggar answers: "I have no shirt."

With an expression of incredulous distaste he floored his inform-
ant, the late Cecil Sprigg of the then *Manchester Guardian,* asking: "You mean to say, in England you eat *five* plates of spaghetti
for lunch, and drink *five* bottles of wine?" Instead of five times
better off, the English appeared to him as gluttonously eating and
drinking five times more than can be harmonized with the essence
of civilized living.

What was overlooked by both parties, however, was that the
Italian standard was not necessarily lower than the British but
different and cheaper, and that, as long as the various communities cultivate different modes of life, and have different concepts
of perfection and serenity, living-standard comparisons have
meaning only if made not *between* communities but *within* communities. A rational appraisal of the position of living levels in
Loiza Aldea must therefore be expressed in terms and targets that
make sense in Loiza Aldea, not in Boston, just as a vegetarian
standard of eating can be appraised only within its own frame of
reference, in terms of the better or worse preparation of combinations of vegetables, not in terms of adding meat.

Only when different communities begin chasing the same
worldly idols can the achievements of each be defined in terms
of the other. It is therefore quite proper to compare the living
levels of the Soviet Union with those of the United States. For
the levels of both are rungs of the same ladder, as we can see
from the admitted ambition of the communist world first to
reach, then to rival, and finally to surpass the United States. It is
therefore no paradox that the American dream of the good life
should be the target of both, with the only difference that the
communist materialists think they can attain it faster than the
money-minded capitalist materialists.

But the same dream is not necessarily shared by other communities. It is not by Loiza Aldea (or rather, it *was* not. For the
spirit of universal brotherhood has at least succeeded in subdu-
ing the spirit of local identity there also, turning what should
have been perfected as a sylvan composition in bamboo and wood
into the slum-breeding graft of alien cubby-hole concrete).[1]

---

[1] Friends sometimes are shocked at hearing me call Loiza Aldea—a sylvan
composition in bamboo full of enchanting half naked children playing under

Nor is it as yet shared by a number of underdeveloped regions in other countries, to judge by their frantic efforts to protect themselves against the destruction of their identity at the hand of an indiscriminately 'outward-looking" industrialization. And as long as it is not shared, it makes as little sense to persuade these countries to develop within the high-cost context of the Russo-American dream as it would to suggest to curly black beauties to wear their hair as straight as whites; to whites to tan their skins until they look as dark as blacks, or to generals to wear their medals and other military adornments as women do, in the imaginative form of bracelets and necklaces designed by Oscar de la Renta rather than the pedantic alignments of military geometry.

THE LOW COST OF GOOD TASTE. ARCHITECT HENRY KLUMB'S ELEGANT PUERTO RICAN HOME IS BUILT FROM THE SAME MATERIAL FROM WHICH THE LOWLIEST SLUM HUT IS BUILT.

palm trees near the ever rolling surf of the shimmering Atlantic—paradisical. But how do we envision paradise? As mid-town Manhattan full of traffic jams, nightclubs, neon lights, restaurants, top hatted revellers, Dior-dressed ladies, bank presidents, Cadillacs, service clubs, beauty parlours, health clinics? Or as a sylvan composition in bamboo full of naked beauties playing under palm trees on the shimmering beaches near the ever rolling surf of time?

Chapter Four

BIKINI STANDARD OF LIVING

*Luxury here takes a turn much more
towards enjoyment than consumption.*

—ARTHUR YOUNG, ON VENICE

WHAT would be the advantage of underdeveloped countries effecting their development within a native frame of
reference in the place of the currently pursued way of
international standardization? In the first place, as I have already
suggested, it would render development so cheap that it could
be financed locally. All it would need is the proper organization
and application of the available under-utilized supply of labour,
just as all the English bourgeois needs to finance a splendid rock
garden is to liquefy his congealed labour power by getting off the
couch. And secondly, as the Renaissance city-states showed
long before tractors, cars, or railroads were invented, a "nativist"
development spells of course neither retardation nor primitivism.
On the contrary. It is capable of the most sophisticated culmination considering that the material that goes into the huts of a
tropical village can also be assembled in the form of mansions.

But to get the idea across to our modern nation builders, they
must first be made to realize that, as there are differences
between, there are also differences *within,* standards of living.
Then they will understand that the simplest way of raising the
levels of any given standard is not by switching to an imported
variety dependent on values shaped outside the native tradition,
but by ascending the rungs of the local standard as they naturally
arrange themselves one above the other within the heretofore
neglected framework of a long familiar pattern. In other words,
the simplest development method for Trinidad is to rise in
Trinidadian, not American, fashion; for Cuba to proceed on
Cuban, not on Russian legs; for Martinique to become a better

Martinique, not a greater France; for Antigua a sunnier Antigua, not a linear descendent of good gray fog-bound England. If this is dismissed by so many contemporary development statesmen and common-marketeers as romantic nonsense or a callous subterfuge for prolonging imperialist exploitation, it can be explained only if they themselves have so little confidence in the taste of their own peoples as to be convinced that the Cuban, Trinidadian, or Antiguan ways of life would even in their perfection amount to nothing as compared to the marvels the detested American suburb can offer.

Speaking more concretely: What exactly would an unassisted, unaffiliated development, carried out within the local framework of every region's own resources and habits, mean in terms of the four basic ingredients of the good life—food, clothing, housing and social convivium?

1. *Food standards* would be improved through emphasis on quantity, quality, and culinary preparation, not through a change in its basic composition. A native rice-bean-fish standard would become a better rice-bean-fish, not a foreign and dearer meat-carrot-pea, standard. Luxury, as the 18th-century traveller Arthur Young observed when comparing the seemingly poorer life of Venice with that of his native England already reaping the first fruit of the Industrial Revolution, would take a turn "more towards enjoyment than consumption. The sobriety of the people does much, the nature of their food more; pastes, macaroni, and vegetables are much easier provided than beef and mutton. Cookery, as in France, enables them to spread a table for half the expense of an English one,"[1] and perhaps twice as tasty.

2. *Dress standards* would be improved by adjusting design to local environment rather than to the tone set by Prince Philip or Christian Dior. If the Romans could be elegant without the expense of a tie, and more comfortable in addition, why should Africans or West Indians not do likewise? And if women look lovely in bikinis on Caribbean beaches, why should a modified material-saving bikini-standard not be extended inland?[2] Nor

---

[1] Arthur Young. *Travels in France and Italy.* Everyman's Library, No. 720, pp. 254-5.

[2] The mini-skirt has done exactly that—in the rich *developed* countries!

is there a reason why tropical men should not find masculine ways of dressing in shorts, loin cloth, or breezy toga instead of drain-pipe trousers; or wear uncostly sandals instead of shoes designed for Wall-Street bankers? They need but overcome the prejudice that loin cloths and sandals are effeminate. Gandhi liberated India in loin cloth, not in dinner jacket. And the world has been conquered in sandals twice: by Roman soldiers and the Apostles of Christ.

3. *Housing standards.* What applies to dress, applies also to shelter. For as houses can be erected expensively with unfamiliar imported methods and equipment, they can also be built cheaply simply by making people assemble the material around them in the form of sturdy homes rather than shacks. One of the most beautiful, most distinguished, most comfortable, most serene, most airy, most elegant, and most tropical of tropical country houses is the Puerto Rican home of the architect Henry Klumb. Yet, as its owner likes to stress with justified pride, it contains not an ounce of stuff of which the huts of the lowliest slum dwellers are not also made. All it required was taste. And taste is free.

4. *Convivium.* Finally, as far as a healthy *communal convivium* is concerned: the uneconomical way of trying to improve it is by regressing in contemporary fashion from a slow pedestrian to a fast motorized existence with all the abomination this entails in suburbanization, urban sprawl, traffic jams, trade strangulation, pollution, accident, loss of identity, destruction of the spirit of both village and city life and, above all, in costs of such astronomical magnitudes that the mere appraisal of traffic difficulties in a minor conurbation such as Acra or San Juan has been budgeted with a cool million dollars. On the other hand, if the social convivium is improved within the context of the local environment, it would again prove so uncostly that it could be afforded by every community itself. All that is needed is to concentrate planning energies not on the waste of expansion but on the economy of urban contraction. This would automatically bring the cost of everything, from sewage disposal and street-cleaning to mass movement and transportation, as geometrically down as expansion pushes it up.

Instead of dissipating resources in highway construction, improvement could then be much more simply achieved by stressing the preservation of pedestrian proportions. Instead of creating nerve-wrecking commuter-ridden sprawls, it would build communities of greater density but less tension. It would, in other words, restore the principal amenity that induced people to choose life in cities in the first place: the absence of distances resulting from the compact interlaced arrangement of all commercial, professional, educational, and convivial activities in the midst of the same residential neighbourhood.

The symbol of standards perfected in the native style is therefore not, as is often believed, the voodoo politician with fly-whisk, top hat, grass skirt, wood alcohol, and slum hut. It is the sophistication of Florence, the music of Salzburg, the architecture of Venice, the sacral character of Toledo, the grace of San Juan (the native city, that is), the house of Henry Klumb, the dinner table of Normandy, the pub in the Cotswold village of Slad.

Moreover, the kind of perfection this represents is not only by far the cheapest; domestically, it is also by far the most acceptable alternative. True, the heady new brand of Peking, Moscow, Oxford, or Yale-bred native leaders may no longer be able to do without a scotch at 5, dress uniform at 7, yacht for cocktails at weekends, Rolls Royce for the importance of looking earnest, jets for living it up with Commissars, Kings, and Christine Keeler, and bronze for monuments to the glory of themselves.[1] But what counts is the people. And while all are impatient to live better according to their own taste, they have yet to show any particular anxiety for following their moon-struck leaders into the speedy russo-anglosaxonifaction of their style of life. They still prefer Porto Fino to Puerto Nuevo, and Rio de Janeiro to Brasilia.

---

[1] The condition is well described by the term "squandermania," which Dahomey rioters hurled at President Hubert Maga whose Western tastes, "notably the magnificent palace he built himself for $3,000,000," (*Time,* November 8, 1963), ultimately led to his downfall.

Chapter Five

SELF-SUFFICIENCY VERSUS SPECIALIZATION IN ECONOMIC THEORY

Rendez-nous à nous mêmes.
—ANTOINE DE MONTCHRETIEN
TO THE KING OF FRANCE

I F I have succeeded in conveying that self-reliant unassisted development aiming at a high degree of self-sufficiency does not necessarily lead to reactionary primitivism, why has economic theory been opposed to it for nearly 200 years? Already Adam Smith listed as one of the five prerequisites of a maximum increase in the wealth of nations not a limited national but an unrestricted free world market. For the greater the specialization of labour, the greater becomes labour's productivity; and the wider the market, the more is it possible for labour to specialize. Hence Smith's idea of turning the entire world into a common market.

The theoretical support of this proposition rests mainly on the classical *law of comparative advantage* which shows compellingly how a nation can increase its riches by abandoning all-round self-sufficiency in favour of specializing in those fields where its labour is comparatively more productive than in other fields. For by exporting its surplus production from its specialized fields, it is able to exchange it for much greater quantities of the goods, whose domestic production it has sacrified, than it could have obtained had it produced also these other goods itself. A popular class room illustration of the principle pictures a lawyer who is at the same time the champion typist of his town. No one is able to type better than he. Yet, he will earn a very much higher income if, instead of self-sufficiently doing both his legal *and* secretarial work himself, he purchases typing services from an outsider while concentrating his own labour on his legal activities in which it is comparatively much more productively and, hence, lucratively employed than in secretarial work.

Another powerful argument against the idea of pushing economic development through self-sufficiency is provided by the historic success of the famous 19th-century ancestor of the contemporary Common Market, the German *Zollverein*. Whatever the experience of the present European Economic Community may in the end demonstrate, at least as regards the *Zollverein*, theorists are unanimously agreed that, without her prior economic unification, Germany could never have become the industrial power she now is.

Granted! But should one give a boy of five a glass of rum simply because, as he points out, it seems to have benefited his father? Both Adam Smith and the early supporters of the *Zollverein* were quite right when they theorized that a free world market for England in the one case, and a free intra-German market in the other, would give their national economies a tremendous boost. But what current development theory citing these early examples fails either to mention or to see, is that both England and the German states had by then reached a high level of pre-industrial maturity. Their cities were blossoming, their patterns set, their identity established, their universities flourishing, their economies thriving.[1]

The cause pushing them towards greater integration and union was therefore not that they were underdeveloped back waters in the contemporary sense, but that they were just advancing from the *manu*facturing to the *machino*facturing mode of production which, with its suddenly increased productivity, was indeed

---

[1] Nothing shows the thriving condition of pre-Zollverein regional economies better than the joyful welcome with which the trading world greeted the abolition of customs boundaries at the opening hour of the year 1834. As an eyewitness told decades later, "Long trains of wagons stood at the high roads, which till then had been cut up by tax barriers. At the stroke of midnight, every turnpike was thrown open, and amid cheers the waggons hastened over the boundaries, which they could henceforth cross in perfect freedom. Everyone felt that a great object had been attained." (*The Zollverein*. By W. O. Henderson. Chicago: Quandrangle Books, 1960, p. 375). Obviously there could have been no "long train of wagons" laden with goods dashing across boundaries, had the economies furnishing them not already reached a high level of development *before* their merger.

dependent on larger than local markets. But significantly, since the German states were half a century behind England in reaching their pre-industrial maturity, they established their *Zollverein* in 1834 likewise with a lag of half a century, seeking wider markets not when England felt ready to withstand the competitive rigours of free trade but when they themselves had sufficiently matured. And even after 1834, when they stepped from manufacturing maturity to machinofacturing adolescence, the freedom of their common market applied only to the limits of the *Zollverein* (the future national territory of Germany), until attainment of their full industrial maturity permitted them at last, by 1867, to join the grown-up world of free traders. Prior to that moment, they not only abstained from following England's tempting example of seeking prosperity through free-trading world markets but, like the equally lagging United States, actually cut themselves off in protectionist isolation, as befits the adolescent mercantilist phase of nation building.

Hence, economic theory which, induced by the *law of comparative advantage,* supports specialization, industrialization, free trade, and common markets, is unexceptionable. But it is not valid for all phases of development. It presupposes pre-industrially fully matured and socially fully developed countries. Applied to underdeveloped areas it has the same effect as the glass of rum has on the boy of five. It does not pep up. It intoxicates. This is why, as long as England or the German states were underdeveloped, their economic theorists were not free traders but protectionists, suggesting the same policies I have sketched in the preceding chapters: a maximum of muscle-strengthening foundation-cementing self-sufficiency, and an increase in both the wealth of their nations and the living standards of their citizens through the unaided, unaffiliated mobilization of their domestic resources.

The name under which the body of theory adapted to this preparatory, nation-building phase of 18th and 19th century economic development became known was cameralism, mercantilism, economic nationalism, or neo-mercantilism (if, as in the United States, it was contemporaneous with the free-trade doctrines advocated by the classical school of an already matured England). And it is *this* body of theory that must be applied to the underdeveloped countries passing today through their mer-

Self-Sufficiency Versus Specialization in Economic Theory

cantilist phase of economic growth, not the "advanced" economics now taught in Oxford, Harvard, or Moscow to fit the latter's own advanced environments. Those whose ground is not yet set should be shown how to build on stilts, not in concrete which will just make them sink.

For this reason, countries which in the past applied principles such as the famous *law of comparative advantage,* which presupposed economic advance, on the assumption that they were advanced economic principles, did not benefit from the superior efficiency offered by their specialization but fell victim to the very condition that perpetuated their retardation—the dreaded rise of over-specialized lopsided one-crop economies. The only way by which early American leaders averted falling into a similar trap was by insisting that the advanced economics of the much admired Smithian England was all wrong and that, as far as *they* were concerned, proper growth depended on the opposite of what the *law of comparative advantage* implied: protection, diversification, and self-sufficiency, even if this meant the building up of temporarily less efficient industries.[1]

---

[1] The outsanding representative of early American protectionism was Henry Charles Carey (1793-1879), whose "peculiarly American Economy" Alexander Gray lists as "the supreme example of the truth that the economist reflects his environment." Carey distinguishes between commerce (interchange within a community) which he approves, and trade (interchange between communities) against which he warns. The class serving the one, he pictures as "desiring to effect exchanges *with* their fellow-men, and thus maintaining commerce; while the other desires to effect exchanges *for* them, and thus to perform acts of trade." Arguing for the protection of the former and the rejection of the latter, he proceeds to show that "the first tends, as has been seen, to the promotion of perfect steadiness in the motion of society; whereas increase in the other tends necessarily to the production of what is called 'gluts'—the trader finding it profitable so to act, as to cause those changes in the prices of labour and of commodities which enable him to buy cheaply and sell dearly," (*Principles of Social Science.* Philadelphia: J. P. Lippincott, 1869, Vol. III p. 44).

Some of Carey's other arguments for contracted and protected local economies are summarized by Gray in *The Development of Economic Doctrine* (London: Longmans, Green, & Co., 1957, pp. 258-259) in the following terms: "Protection promotes concentration; Free Trade dispersion. Protection is competition for the purchase of labour; Free Trade for the sale of labour. As war is encouraged if men are cheap, Free Trade encourages war. Free

Development Without Aid

In other words, though America's cameralist neo-mercantilism may have appeared theoretically retarded to a classically enlightened England, for a retarded United States it offered the only philosophy leading ultimately to the latter's dramatic advance. Moreover, the compelling story of the lawyer and his secretary notwithstanding, specialization along the lines set by the *law of comparative advantage* is a virtue only up to a point even in mature economies. It is the same as with individuals. I may be a better teacher than a cook, and should therefore mainly take to teaching rather than cooking. Yet, as we all know, I may be a still better teacher, and certainly a happier individual, if I practice also a little cooking, building, car fixing, carpentry, and plumbing on the side, rather than getting helplessly stuck as a specialized and stupefied one-track genius in a surrounding swamp of ignorance. This is why the most sensible education tries to develop us as rounded-off, self-sufficient universal men rather than as specialized experts depending in every step we make on the assistance of the whole human brotherhood. Is there a reason why what we welcome in the education of men should not be welcome in the development of nations?

Trade again stands for distant markets; Protection for the home market; but those who seek distant markets are separated from their wives and children, spend much time on the road and in taverns, and are thus liable to be led into dissipation. Free Trade thus stands for the dissipation of the tavern; Protection for the blessedness of the home."—Not that I subscribe to all of Carey's reasons for protection as he lists them in his *Harmony of Interests* (p. 52). But his main conclusion, that it saves an underdeveloped community the transport burdens of great distance, is as valid today as it was then.

Chapter Six

THE *CUV* APPROACH

There is wisdom in smallness, if only on account of the smallness and patchiness of human knowledge, which relies on experience far more than on understanding.

—Schumacher

WHAT I have emphasized in the foregoing is the advantage gained by using protected cameralist self-sufficiency as the logical first step on the road towards economic development. This should however not be interpreted as precluding the *subsequent* widening of markets or the fusion of neighbouring economies, if their gregarious leaders should ultimately so desire. It merely means that the components to be fused must first have reached their individual maturity and identity singly. After that, the argument against their union may become as irrelevant as the argument against marriage once the children wanting it have fully developed. But as in marriage, the soundest condition for success of a non-authoritarian pluralist society rests even after fusion on each of the partners retaining a large measure of self-sufficient independence, lest the difficulties or demise of one ruin the chances of all.

Nor does my emphasis on self-sufficency preclude industrialization. All it means is a different *type* of industrialization, and a different composition of the resultant national product. It will always make sense to preserve, at a *reduced* scale, a few foreign-exchange earning industries operating not only with comparative but absolute advantage. A case in point is the production of sugar, coffee, rum, or bananas in tropical countries. But aside from these, the best way to build up a developing economy is with a view towards diversification, and the intensification of a geographically limited domestic economy in depth, rather than by adjusting it to the unreliable oceanic magnitudes of transport-dominated international specialization. In this way it becomes possible to invest at an early stage the available capital in consumer-goods industries where it can contribute to meaningful enrichment, rather than having to let it congeal in the permafrost of transport,[1] distribution, integration, and other remedial commodities such as trucks, jets or ships, which are needed for servicing a large market, but do not add an iota to the citizens' good life.

True, this shift in emphasis away from integration and distribution commodities towards an early development of consumer goods industries, such as is possible only in small societies unburdened by the tyranny of distances and scale, will lead to a proportionate reduction in total attainable national product—an aggregate that makes no distinction between a bottle of transmission oil and a bottle of wine. But it will not effect the chance of increasing on this very ground the more important aggregate of personal consumption. On the contrary. The dispensability of transmission oil will enable a grown-up society to have more, not less, wine. And the saving in trucks bringing caviar from Russia will provide us not with a poorer but a richer table closer at hand. The reason for this is the same that explains why the diminished need for elevator space tends to make living space per family not scarcer but ampler in smaller buildings than in sky-scrapers; or why the renunciation of commuting by automobile furnishes the "victim" not with less but more leisure provided, of course, that he contracts at the same time his field of operation by moving his workshop back close to his home.

---

[1] Similar to one of my own principal arguments, Henry Charles Carey has based his entire case for contracted, protected, internationally uninvolved, self-sufficient economic development on the proposition, glaringly affecting all market-distant underdeveloped countries, that "the first and heaviest tax to be paid by land and labour is that of transportation." He recommends, therefore, a policy that insures the concentrated establishment of all complimentary economic activities within the narrow confines of the same geographic region, causing "the loom and the anvil to take their natural places by the side of the plough and the harrow." As Gray says (*op. cit.*, p. 258); "most of his arguments, indeed, are but variants to this fundamental contention that 'the object of Protection is that of diminishing the distance and the waste between the producer and the consumer.' " It goes without saying that Carey's argument is directed not against the intermediary mechanism of "commerce" but against the impoverishing transportation costs of "trade" too far flung.

HOW MANY MILES IN A LOAF OF BREAD?

The publicity picture of a trucking firm does not answer the question it puts. It merely states that "It takes many elements to produce the ingredients that go into a loaf of bread—and that the common denominator is transportation. Nevertheless, it shows dramatically the validity of Henry Charles Carey's dictum that "the first and heaviest tax to be paid by land and labour is that of transportation," and that a better way of pushing progress is not by far-flung, mileage-devouring international integration supporting tractors and trailers, but through contracted economies, with "the loom and anvil to take their natural places by the side of the plough and harrow." (p. 40).—For more of Carey's ideas, see pp. 37n.-38n., 185, 189.

HOW MANY RICHES IN BREAD WITHOUT MILES?

Self-sufficiency in the place of a transport economy may not lower the price of bread. But its savings in the consumption of senseless mileage costs supports a richer type of progress. Instead of trailers, trailers, tractors, vans, and trailers, it makes possible more spacious houses, urban adornments, stately inns, engaging city-scapes, and other indispensable accessories of a civilized standard of living. To have an idea of the retarding effect of excessive transport dependence we need but look at a congressional study released on April 15, 1965. This reveals a 15% drop in prices received by the farmer in the preceding 17 years, while the retail prices paid by the consumer jumped by 31% during the same period. The obvious explanation: the savings of scale achieved in production were cancelled out by more than twice their amount through the increase in the costs of transportation made necessary by large-scale integration. (p. 40).

NOTES FOR FOLLOWING PAGES

HOW MANY MILES IN A LOAF OF BREAD?

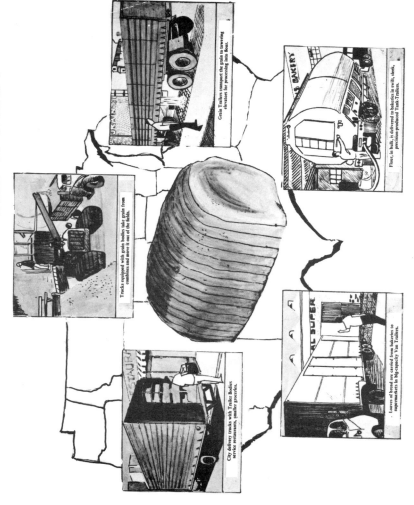

Grain Trailers transport the grain to towering elevators for processing into flour.

Flour, in bulk, is delivered to bakeries in swift, sleek, precision-produced Tank-Trailers.

Trucks equipped with grain bodies take grain from combines and move it out of the fields.

City delivery trucks with Trailer Bodies service restaurants, smaller groceries.

Loaves of bread are carried from bakeries to supermarkets in big-capacity Van Trailers.

HOW MANY RICHES IN BREAD WITHOUT MILES?

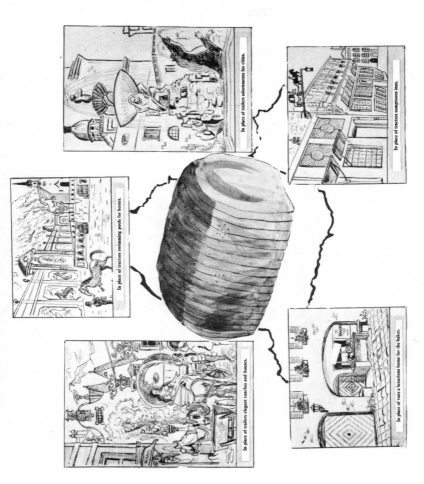

In place of trailers adornments for cities.

In place of tractors sumptuous inns.

In place of tractors swimming pools for horses.

In place of trailers elegant coaches and houses.

In place of vans a luxurious home for the baker.

"HOW ABOUT NIPPING INSIDE AND TELLING THEM
SATURATION DAY HAS ARRIVED?"

The CUV Approach

In other words, a largely self-sufficient domestic economy, servicing a region of limited size intensively, implies a whole set of advantages. In the first place it offers not a diminished but an enlarged output of enjoyable consumer goods at the cost not of more but fewer producer goods than are required in the transport-devouring expanse of common-market economies. Hence the paradoxical possibility for unintegrated small societies to enlarge their net by diminishing their gross; to increase per-capita consumption by actually lowering instead of raising the aggregate of their production.[1]

Secondly, since a small market discourages the development of large enterprise, domestic self-sufficiency implies an industrialization pattern based on small competitive rather than big monopolistic business units. But this again means merely a different, not a more deficient, type of industrialization. 80% of all Swiss firms employ fewer than 50 workers. Yet, far from lagging, Switzerland ranks first amongst the nations of the world with a degree of industrialization of 53.6%, followed by Belgium with 51%, Germany with 49%, Great Britain 47.5%, Sweden 40.5%, and trailed by the United States with 40%, Italy with 36.3% and France with 35%. This shows conclusively that large size, whether of market or enterprise, has in itself little

[1] The point has been elaborated by me both conceptually and statistically in a number of studies such as *Toward a New Measurement of Living Standards*, The American Journal of Economics and Sociology, October 1955; *The Asprin Standard*, Business Quarterly, Summer 1956; in Chapter 8 of *The Breakdown of Nations*, New York: Rinehart, 1957; and Chapter 3 of *Die Ueberentwickelten oder Die Gefahr der Grösse*, Dusseldorf: Econ Verlag, 1962. To quote from the latter: analyzing changes in the United States "in total personal consumption in relation to changes in gross national product between 1939 and 1951," when by my calculations America pushed beyond the point of optimum social size, "it is interesting to see that relative to the increasing rate of increasing national product the rate of consumption increase was declining and that, since 1944, the two have actually begun to move inversely, showing *increasing* total personal consumption only when national product, as a result of attempted reduction of national power, was temporarily *reduced* through curtailment of government spending." See statistical tables and diagrams in *op. cit.*

t) do with either the intensity or the degree of industrialization.[1]

And thirdly, the natural small-firm pattern of an Owenite kind of local self-sufficiency provides the economy with the same counter-cyclical resiliency as four-wheel independent suspension imparts to the stability of a car. Or to use another image, it has the same moderating effect on the amplitude of cylical fluctuations which a system of dykes or small harbours exerts on the heaving water masses of the open seas. By dividing instead of uniting, it does not impede contacts with the world around. But as the dyke-like small-peasant structure of France has so often demonstrated in the past, it prevents disturbances such as recessions from linking up their separate momentum in the dreaded chain reaction of tidal waves which are able to reach destructive proportions only in the integrated oceans of unified economies of large scale.

For all this, even "progressive" economic theory—which, as all modern social theory, is prevented from absorbing the essence of today by being kept too busy codifying the conditions of yesterday—is, in spite of fashionable common-market mythology and the logic of the laws of comparative and absolute advantage, no longer quite so opposed to local self-sufficiency (as a development target preceding interregional integration) as the slow swings of its staid academic momentum might indicate.

I have already mentioned the eminent "radical" English economist and top adviser of the Labour Party, Thomas Balogh of Oxford, as a witness warning against the pitfalls of economic union. Similarly, on the more conservative side, one might cite the equally eminent Harvard economist Gottfried von Haberler (who has the distinction of holding one of the rare baronies of the Principality of Liechtenstein) as an early theoretical opponent of the Common Market at a time when I myself was still looking into the opposite direction; or the distinguished holder of the

---

[1] I hope I shall be forgiven for not bringing these figures from 1960, gleaned from Austin Robinson's *Economic Consequences of the Size of Nations* (London: Macmillian, 1960, p. 54 pp.), up to date to reflect the early 1970's. Since this is a discussion of societies in development, which is a historic process, the possibly changed figures of today will not invalidate the message conveyed by figures collected at a different transit point.

Chair of Marshall and Pigou, James Meade of Cambridge, who is anything but enthusiastic about the prospect of seeing Great Britain sucked into the bloodstream of the European Economic Community.

Also mentioned in this context must be the powerful arguments in favour of small rather than large-scale development implied in Gunnar Myrdal's *Theory of Circular and Cumulative Causation,*[1] and Prebisch's *Law of Increasing Peripheral Neglect,* or the penetrating writings of the United Nations economist Hans Singer, who advocates small-scale "guerilla tactics" of development in preference to the inefficient conventional methods of massive "frontal attack."[2] But pride of place must be given to Dr. E. F. Schumacher, the inspired former Director of Statistics of Britain's National Coal Board who, in his earlier years, supplied Maynard Keynes with some of the latter's most effective ammunition.[3] But he has long since established himself as the most eloquent as well as the most conscious exponent of what he calls the *Theory of Intermediate Technology* which stresses both the superior development efficiency of simpler over the most advanced methods of production, as well as the general organizational advantages which territorially small economies have over integrated large ones.[4]

Another sign of the rising significance of the idea of small units as the cure of the cancer of social overgrowth is the emergence in all corners of the world not only of individual theorists but of entire movements trying to give expression to their hunches with

[1] See footnote 2 on p. 22.

[2] See particularly his *International Development—Growth and Change.* New York: McGraw-Hill, 1964.

[3] Schumacher is among others the author of the paper "Multilateral Clearing" (*Economica,* Spring 1943) which Keynes used almost verbatim in his composition of the famous White Paper which appeared a few days later under the title "Plan for an International Clearing Union."

[4] As economic Adviser respectively of the British Control Commission in Germany, the National Coal Board, the Government of Burma, and the Indian Planning Commission, Dr. Schumacher was particularly well placed for drawing his theories not only from speculation but a wide base of practical experience. See among many others his *"Intermediate Technology,"* "Industrial Society," "Buddhist Economics," in *Resurgence,* Vol. 1, Nos. 2, 3, and 11; and *"The New Economics,"* in Vol. 2, No. 3.

new kinds of communitarian proposals. Many of them are not unlike those of Robert Owen's famous *Report to the County of Lanark* of 1821 in which he suggested, as the best way for relieving the economic distress following the Pan-European conquests of Napoleon, the spanning of the world with a network of *Parallelograms* and self-sufficient *Villages of Co-operation* on the model of his own brilliantly successful New Lanark.[2] A similar thought is echoed in contemporary Great Britain by movements such as the *Fourth World,* whose principal magazine, *Resurgence,* states as "its starting aim the repudiation of existing power structures, not because they are Capitalist or Communist or Fascist or whatever, but simply because they are too big."[3] In Italy, the theme is taken up by the "groups-within-groups" ideas of the eloquent Sicilian reformer Danilo Dolci; and in India, by the Gandhi-inspired *Gramdan* movement of Vinoba Bhave, "India's Walking Saint," which aims at reconstructing the enormous subcontinent by turning the current centralized monster state into 700,000 self-sufficient Village Republics, of which tens of thousands have already been set up.[4]

---

[2] Robert Owen was dismissed, most famously in Marx's *Communist Manifesto,* as a utopian. Yet nothing demonstrated better than his own New Lanark how high living standards and high wages could be achieved on a small scale in the midst of the abject misery then prevailing among the big, both factories and communities. He has found a contemporary duplication in Ernest Bader's equally successful factory-community of Wollaston, Northamptonshire. See: *Work and Community—the Scott-Bader Commonwealth and the Quest for a New Social Order. By Fred H. Blum. London: Routledge & Kegan Paul, 1968.*

[3] As John Papworth and Roger Franklin, the spirited editors of *Resurgence,* write: "We envisage a Fourth World where government and economics are under genuine human control because the size of such units are small, sensible, and human-scale, where there is a maximum of decentralized decision making, and where the pace of change is regulated not by the appetites of an overmighty minority for profit and power but by the day-to-day needs of small-scale human communities and the psychic capacities of their members to adapt."

[4] See Vinoba Bhave, *"Atomic Age Independence;"* A. C. Sen, *"Gramdan,"* in *Resurgence,* Vol. 1, No. 12, and Vol. 2, Nos 8/9. Also: *Non-Violence or Non-Existence. By Satish Kumar. London: Christian Action, 1969; and A Great Society of Small Communities. By Sugata Dasgupta. London: Housmans, 1969.*

The CUV Approach

All of these movements are inexorably nudged on: *administratively,* by the gradual reversal of the intellectual tide away from integration in the direction of "devolution." Witness such heretofore centralized countries as Italy, which has already begun to devolve power to the 20 "autonomous regions" envisaged in the constitution, or Great Britain, where the vision of a federally or confederally Disunited rather than United Kingdom is no longer quite so shocking as it once was.[1] And *academically,* we see the trend in the emergence of research centres such as the Philadelphia-based *Regional Science Association,* which has recently begun to spread its conceptual wings over widening areas of the underdeveloped world.

The latter may or may not declare itself openly in support of the development value of nativism, regionalism, and self-sufficiency as opposed to the foreign-aid, mutual-assistance, and common-market alternatives of economic advance. Before it is possible to tell, its MIT-inspired high priests will first have to step out of the darkened sanctum of their prestigious mathematical encrustation into the cold no-nonsense light of de-mystified prose. However, even in the absence of a declaration of intent, it would be incongruous if their conclusions would fail to bear out the regionalism of their title. At least none of the participants of the First Latin American Regional Science Congress (Caracas 1960) objected to my suggestion that their range of equations and methods should be extended by the inclusion of the *CUV* approach. Nor was there any objection when I translated this impressively austere code word, *conçu et verbalisé par moi même,*

[1] Aside from the lively Celtic nationalist movements that have recently sprung up particularly in Wales under the inspired leadership of Gwynfor Evans whose party, Plaid Cymru, aims for a *Britannic Confederation* of independent national and regional states, Britain's Liberal Party has also declared itself in favour of setting up independent regional parliaments, and even the centralist Labour Party called on a Royal Commission in October 1968 to appraise the possibility of relinquishing some powers to the regions. One British plan conceives of the establishment of 40 to 30 "city-regions," just one inch short of "city-states," and another, submitted by a Labour M.P., J. P. Mackintosh, suggests in *Devolution of Power* (Penguin, 1968), the setting up of a total of 11 regional parliaments in Great Britain which would create several governments on the soil of even England herself.

as Sacha Guitry would have put it, as *Contraction to Uninstrumented Visibility.*

Decoded, this means what I have been advocating throughout these pages: a return to the development approach of the Renaissance city-states. If they succeeded so spectacularly, it was simply because their territories were contracted to dimensions that could be mastered by ordinary mortals without the need of complicated theoretical instruments and statistical radar screens. Adjusted in size to the small stature that God has given us, their problems could therefore by nature never outgrow the genius of their local leaders, or the resources of their natural endowment.[1]

There is only one drawback to the *CUV* approach which might justify groups such as the Regional Science Association to keep on shrouding their findings in the shadows of mathematical formulae and alphabetical abbreviations. This is that, once they have achieved a region's contraction to the dimensions most conducive to unaided development, the need for their services diminishes in proportion to their very achievement. They become disposable. And for high-salaried outside advisers this is as hard to accept as the prescription of Dr. Marx to high-powered communist rulers to start withering away with the advent of socialism, to whose attainment they are committed, but whose realization deprives them of both their mission and job. Yet, there is no other way out. When the promised land is reached, the leader of the march loses his function.

---

[1] No one has reasoned the reduction of the size of states to fit the small stature of man more excellently than Aristotle when he writes: "A great city is not to be confounded with a populous one. Moreover, experience shows that a very populous city can rarely, if ever, be well governed; since all cities which have a reputation for good government have a limit of population. We may argue on grounds of reason, and the same result will follow. For law is order, and good law is good order; but a very great multitude cannot be orderly: to introduce order into the unlimited is the work of divine power—of such power as holds together the universe." *(Politics* 1326a). And a little further he gives the most precise definition of *CUV* proportions when he writes: "Clearly then the best limit to the population of a state is the largest number which suffices for the purposes of life, and can be taken in at a single view." *(Ibid.,* 1326b).

Chapter Seven

CUV AND THE URBAN COMMON MARKET

*A great city is not to be confounded
with a populous one.*
            —ARISTOTLE

WHAT is true of modern nation building is true also of modern city building. A look at the latter may therefore offer a valuable analogy for shedding additional light on the complexities of the former. For also in the case of cities, the chief problem is not solved but caused by the uneconomical integration of communities, which ought to have remained separate, into the interlaced traffic-ridden unity of an expanding urban common market. Therefore, the solution lies also here in the *CUV* approach: that is the application of a high measure of cost-saving contraction and introspective polynuclear localism not only to the whole *of a* city, but also to the separate districts and boroughs *within a city.*

To put it differently; as in the case of nations, sound urban evolution requires a pluralist development in which a maximum of daily concerns, instead of being *integrated,* are *duplicated* in a variety of self-contained, closely packed rival centres needing a minimum of joint administration and road-jamming intra-city movement. And just as a good condominium is one in which the various families spend the bulk of their time in the privacy of their separate apartments rather than in the social utility space allotted to their common use such as lobbies, corridors, or elevators; so a good city is one whose inhabitants spend the bulk of their time in the restful enclosure of their local square, rather than in urban traffic corridors and commuter vehicles traversing them. For the very meaning of the square is that it is a focus where, as in one's apartment, all that is needed is close by.

Instead of remaining far-flung semi-rural aggregations of suburban dormitories, cities must therefore once again contract into real cities—dense, close, exciting, sophisticated, elegant, econo-mical, time-saving, pedestrian. If this is done, the most taxing of modern urban problems—commuting in a convivium whose very founding purpose was to save man the agony of commuting— would be solved with the stroke of a pen. And it would be as uncostly as the development of native in the place of international standards of living. For every problem of expansion is automati-cally liquidated by the savings of contraction.

The main question then is this: How can cities be contracted in practical terms? How can the citizen be induced to stay close to his centre, his native square? The answer is not too difficult. All that must be done is to deprive him not of the *means* but of the *motive* for going elsewhere. And to achieve this, three conditions must be fulfilled.

1. The majority of targets of his daily activities—church, school, inn, market, office, side-walk café, theatre, city-hall— must again be closely grouped around his square of residence. As in the case of the Queen of England, the President of the United States or the Governor of Puerto Rico, the supreme status symbol must once again become: to live where one works, and work where one lives.

2. In addition to its utilitarian function as domicile and working place the square must satisfy our aesthetic needs. Like beauty in a woman, this is indeed the chief reason that stops us from running around. Hence, the square must be adorned. Its houses must offer beauty singly, and harmony collectively. And in addition to physical, it must have social, beauty. As the organs of the body, the ingredients of the square must not only all be there, but arranged in proper relationships.

3. As a city expands, it must not swell in cancerous fashion outward from an exploding square, thereby causing its centre to disintegrate and the rest to diffuse. It must grow in biological fashion adding like cells in a body new squares as old ones fill up, each with its own identity, glamour, and patriotism, and with its own magnetic field preventing essentially local movements from developing escape velocities.

The good city must therefore be a mosaic-like federation of a jumble of largely self-sufficient squares breaking up the whole, not an orderly geometrical network of streets tying it together, and choking it to death in the attempt. And by the same token, a good metropolis must be a federation of largely autonomous small cities whose rival beauty does not increase, but prevents, an excess of senseless road-jamming intermingling. Paris, as all ancient capital cities, used to be such a federation with the result that, during the three years I lived there as a student, I travelled to the Champs Elysées not more than five times and to Montmartre perhaps twice—for sight-seeing. For the rest I stayed contentedly in the Latin Quarter. Duplicating in matchless beauty nearly everything that could be found in other districts, this proved seductive enough to keep me, as well as most others, in an innerdirected traffic-reducing pedestrian frame of mind.

A last question is: How can car-loving modern man be induced in practical terms to return to a pedestrian existence? Actually, there exists already a set of modern city-founders achieving precisely this. Applying the *CUV* approach and, like Renaissance princes, operating in competition rather than co-operation, they have long begun to assemble once again the ingredients of the self-sufficient ancient square—residential quarters, restaurants, shops, travel agencies, professional locations, post offices, entertainment facilities, gymnasia, swimming pools, theatres, clubs, religious and educational centres, book stores, art galleries— in the most concentrated of pedestrian space: *The Grand Hotel.* And by stressing aesthetics on top of utility, they have long discovered what still eludes most orthodox planners: that even Americans, supposedly so inseparable from the motorized companionship of their cars, just love it. So much in fact, that one of the problems of tourism in underdeveloped countries is how to get them out of their blissful hotel enclosures to haunt the roads of the hinterlands once more so that also other regions may benefit from their restless dollars.

Thus, the Renaissance idea of self-sufficient contracted local, in the place of far-flung interlaced, development has ceased to be retarded theory and become advanced reality in at least one field. It has been revived with spectacular success by the innkeepers! While old cities are left to die in the quagmire of physical expansion and intellectual orthodoxy, they are busily building in the form of glamourous hotels the new city-states of the future.

Chapter Eight

VELOCITY THEORY OF POPULATION

The fast car is always behind.
—PROVERB

Reduzca la Velocidad y Viva Mas.
—PUERTO RICAN CAR STICKER

THE previous chapters have repeatedly stressed the savings of contracting in contrast to the wastes of expanding economies without offering either theory or figures in support of the proposition. I shall not offer figures as I do not dispose of the assistants needed for compiling them. But I shall submit a theory in an attempt to explain deductively why continued expansion is physically as well as economically self-defeating; why in Malthusian fashion the geometrically rising *costs* of expansion must ultimately outrace the arithmetically rising *returns* of expansion, in the expectation of which they have been incurred.

There is of course the old and elementary *law of diminishing returns* which, as Aristotle noted, puts a limit to the size of everything—plants, animals, implements, firms, markets, cities, states. "For none of these retain their natural power when they are too large or too small, but either wholly lose their nature, or are spoiled."[1] While it is true that the twin *law of variable proportions,* leading to an industrialized mode of production through the substitution of machines for men, permits us to push the barrier set by rising costs beyond its original limits, it is equally true that there is a limit also to the extent to which substitution can be carried on before the industrialization it engenders turns the economies of scale into the diseconomies of unmanagable proportions.[2]

---

[1] Aristotle, Politics, 1326a.

[2] Some idea of the geometrically rising diseconomies of increasing scale can be gained from the fact that, according to an AP report of May 20, 1964,

Velocity Theory of Population

But there is another theory explaining why the increasing costs of expansion must begin to outrace any possible savings of scale at a relatively early stage of growth. Lacking a name, let us call it the *velocity theory of population*. And linking it up with the discussion of the preceding chapter, let us sketch it here with particular reference to problems of urban rather than national expansion, though it applies to the latter as much as to the former.

Assuming then, that we abandon our pedestrian urbanity, and move 1 mile away from the centre of a city expanding on lines of mononuclear integration rather than polynuclear concentration: What will happen?

In the first place, our commuter and transportation costs will increase geometrically to the arithmetic increase in distance caused by our move. For an added mile's journey to our place of work means also an added mile's journey back home, making 2 miles in all. Moreover, if we return home also for lunch, we must cover another 2 miles, bringing the total to 4, or 8 miles if our wife works in town too. However, not only has our place of work become more distant by 1 mile; the same has happened with regard to our market, our school, the church, the theatre, the residences of our friends. In other words, urban expansion by a single mile saddles a family, of let us say four, with multiplied daily *personal* movements totalling perhaps 18 to 20 miles, to say nothing of the corresponding increase in *service* movements gener-

---

"worldwide international trade requires 2.5 trillion pieces of written information annually. In the United States alone, Rep. Graham B. Purcel Jr., (D.-Tex.) estimated that business may spend as much as $111 billion a year on paperwork." Repeating this figure to my students as an example of the shocking cost of paperwork, I listed it as $1.11 billion, making allowance for the obvious misprint. But on re-reading the passage the original figure of $111 billion turned out to be no misprint after all, considering that the sentence immediately following it specified: "That's more than the Federal Budget." I leave it to statisticians to figure out how many houses, schools, supermarkets, hospitals, theatres, factories could be built if this stupendous "paper" sum could be saved. Other items mentioned by Rep. Purcell Jr. transmit the information that, for example, "a questionnaire the Federal Power Commission requires some of the businesses it oversees to fill out . . . weighs 10 pounds, runs to 428 pages and costs some firms as much as $250.000 to answer."

ated by the new suburbs as a result of now vastly expanded garbage-disposal and milk routes, to name but two.

If we further assume that integrated expansion does not stop at 1 mile, but continues to swell outward, we shall not be surprised at the speed with which the same geometric terror rears its head which was brought on the Indian ruler by the inventor of chess. When pressed by his delighted sovereign to name a reward, he asked for no more than a single grain of wheat to be placed on the first square of the chess board, and that the amount be doubled on each successive square. The ruler was disappointed at so modest a request for so marvellous an invention, only to discover that, long before the 64th square was reached, he had lost his kingdom.

The second consequence of integrated expansion is that the newly created added collective distance of 18 or 20 miles per family of four must of course be spanned in approximately the same time as the 2 miles we had to cover as long as we still lived close to the centre of all our activities. This means an acceleration in the velocity of our movement to such an extent that we must change from a pedestrian to a motorized form of transportation. And since motor cars require their own network of roads whose mileage must be adjusted not to the *geographic* distance of our new suburb but to its *use*-distance, which is geographic distance multiplied by the number of movements it has caused, integrated expansion produces an unforeseen added complexity. Instead of bringing outlying districts closer, it paradoxically pushes a suburb from its relatively close *geographic* distance of 1 mile to an *effective* distance of 20 miles, but with the problems of 20 miles compressed into the space of 1.

All this might still be within the intellectual and physical resources of a community were it not for a third consequence, following in the wake of the second but as yet almost totally ignored by urban, economic, and social planners. This is that the increasing velocity imparted to an outward expanding community has the same effect as if the population had grown not only in speed but also in mass, though not a single person may have been added to it numerically. This is the reason which explains why theatres, in addition to normal exits adjusted to audiences moving at ordinary pace, must have in reserve also a number of emergency exits adjusted to audiences moving at an accelerated pace as when under the influence of panic. For just as faster moving particles gain in mass, so do *faster* moving crowds assume the characteristics of *larger* crowds. As a result, theatre exits are considered adequate only if they take into account not the actual *numerical* but the potential *effective* size of an audience, that is numerical size multiplied by speed.

Thus, as increasing geographic distance is, from a traffic point of view, *in effect* multiplied by the number of people negotiating it, the number of people, in turn, is *in effect* multiplied by the increased velocity with which they must move as a result of increased distance. And it is particularly this second multiplier that is responsible not only for the unspeakable increase in the misery of jammed and gassed-up roads following in the wake of every mononuclear, integrated, urban expansion; more importantly it also accounts for our hopeless inability ever again to catch up with traffic problems multiplying at a geometric ratio, while the physical, financial and intellectual resources of even the richest society are at best capable of being enlarged only at an arithmetic ratio.[1]

Every time planners complete engineering marvels such as the futuristic road networks of the splendid city of Caracas, they will therefore discover again and again that, after unveiling the plaques inmortalizing their names, traffic conditions they meant to cure have been aggravated by their very improvements. For

---

[1] Illustrating the implications of the velocity theory of population, the diagrams on p. 56, show the per capita increase in traffic costs for the inhabitants of a town (Pressureville) under three assumptions: (a) rising urban spread; (b) rising urban *physical* population; (c) rising urban *car* population as a result of rising standards of living. Paradoxically, the last condition, brought about by increased productivity, tends to increase per capita traffic costs to such catastrophic dimensions that even the richest community is ultimately unable to bear them. The pauperizing effect of increasing motorized affluence is well illustrated by a random example from the rapidly developing Puerto Rican city of Bayamon which, according to the *San Juan Star* of November 18, 1963 attributes the demise of a prosperous sugar mill to the following causes: "The surprising growth of Bayamon, which has eliminated many of the mill's best lands. The traffic congestion of the city, which makes it prohibitively expensive to transport cane across the city to the mill. The time invested in hauling the cane to the mill is ruinous."

what they overlooked in the case, for example, of the Venezuelan metropolis is that the very speed, which the new urban express highways were supposed to impart to all movement, increased the *actual* size of Caracas from a population of 2 million to an *effective* size of perhaps 10 million, while the roads they added took into account an effective size of at most 2.5 to 3 million.

No wonder that, to the puzzlement of all, the result fell so abysmally short of the target. And no wonder that also in most other cities of the world, the completion of traffic improvement-projects is invariably followed by worsening traffic conditions, caused primarily by the inescapable mass-increasing effect which every increase in velocity exerts on population. Indeed, so important is this factor that with minor exceptions as in India, most contemporary overpopulation problems, both at national and urban levels, make sense as yet only if viewed as cases not of *numerical* but of *velocity* overpopulation, to be dealt with not through birth control or the acquisition of new lands, but through contraction into mass and traffic-reducing forms of denser living. But little can be done about this as long as planners compile their galaxies of figures without recourse to a theory that gives to the velocity factor the same significance socially which has long been accorded to it by physicists in the study of mass, or the quantity theorists of money in the study of inflation.[1]

There seems therefore little need at this juncture for supplementing theory with figures. For a properly formulated *velocity theory of population,* together with the long formulated *law of diminishing returns,* would even in the absence of statistical evidence seem to provide an ample basis for two vital conclusions: 1, that continued development through integrated expansion in nations as well as cities must sooner or later run into financially prohibitive and technically unscalable barriers; and 2, that by dis-

[1] The Quantity Theory of Money shows that, similar to car pressure, the price level is pushed up not only by a *greater* quantity of money (being put in circulation without an appropriately increased volume of goods), but also by the *same* quantity of money being circulated at a *faster* rate. In other words, a smaller amount of money circulating faster has the same effect as a larger amount circulating more slowly, the economically *effective* volume being physical volume times velocity. See my original elaboration of the *velocity theory of population* in *Land Economics,* May 1958, Vol. XXXIV, No. 2.

couraging, rather than providing for, excessive commuter, transportation, and commercial movement, the polynuclear contraction of cities offers at this advanced stage of overgrowth not only the most economical but the *only* practical alternative for improving the scale-bedevilled human condition—all the contrary views of the brotherhood of urban and international integrators notwithstanding.

DIAGRAMS ILLUSTRATING THE MORE THAN PROPORTIONATE INCREASE IN PER-CAPITA TRAFFIC COSTS CAUSED BY URBAN EXPANSION[1]

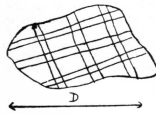

Built-up area criss-crossed by streets
Let us call it Pressureville.
Pressureville has a characteristic diameter D (kilometers). This depends of course on the direction in which we measure D; but it does not change the argument.

I   The total area of Pressureville $= \alpha D^2$, where α depends on shape of town. The average distance people travel in Pressureville to business and supermarkets $= \beta D$.
They spend an average time T travelling (hours).

Their average velocity is approximately $V \sim \dfrac{D}{T}$ (kilometre/hour).

(The sign $\sim$ means it is equal to D/T times some constant which does not concern us here).
The street area of Pressureville $= a^2$ (kilometre square).
This area is populated by n cars; m = average mass of cars.

II *If* these cars just milled around *at random* like *molecules*, they would exert

a pressure $p \sim \dfrac{n.m}{a^2} V$

Car pressure may be defined by the amount of car mass carried through a toll gate of unit width per unit time.

If we combine the expression for p with our earlier expression for $V \sim \dfrac{D}{T}$

we get $p \sim \dfrac{n.m.D^2}{a^2 T^2}$

[1] I am indebted for the mathematical formulation of the Velocity Theory to Professor Eric Kraus, Oceanographic Institute, Woods Hole, Massachusetts.

The unit of $p = \dfrac{\text{number of cars} \times \text{mass}}{\text{time square}}$

When p exceeds critical value px, traffic breaks down and we get a jam.

III We shall now discuss formula (1): Assume people don't like to spend more than a given time (say 1 hour/day) travelling. This then is a constant $T = 1$ hour. However, Pressureville grows. As the town increases, average travel velocity will increase proportionately to the increase in D.

Case (a) D increases, but number and mass of cars remains the same. If car pressure is not to increase, it is necessary to provide new roads at the same rate as D^2 increases: this means D^2/a^2 *must remain constant.*

Case (b) Size of town increases, due to more people coming in. The number of cars per 1,000 people remains however the same. We now have $n \sim D^2$. Therefore, if p is not to increase, D^4/a^2 *must remain constant.*

Case (c) Standard of Living increases. This means both more and bigger cars per 1,000 persons. Then if p is not to increase, D^{4+X}/a^2 *must remain constant.* (x is positive and depends on rise in living standard.)

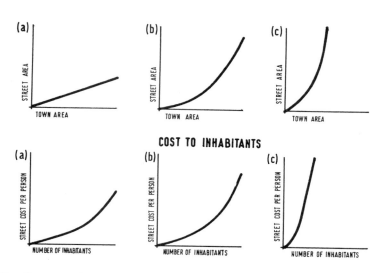

COST TO INHABITANTS

In all cases: (a), (b) and (c), costs per person increase with number of inhabitants. But in case (c), the per capita cost-increase may assume such catastrophic dimensions that even the richest communities are unable to bear it.

Chapter Nine

THE LOW COST OF POVERTY

Poverty sits by the cradle of all our great
men and rocks them up to manhood.
—HEINE

WHEN Cesar Andreu Iglesias, former Secretary General of the Communist Party of Puerto Rico, lost his private job through the courtesy of the Un-American Activities Committee, he could have surrendered to the masochistic joys of self-righteous grief. Instead, he withdrew to a remote mountain top and, by means of rice-and-bean nourished direct-labour finance, built single-handedly a house within less than six months. Had he resorted to bank-nourished indirect money-finance, it would have required either the looting of his party treasury, or the slow accumulation of savings from at least five years of high-salaried bourgeois employment such as Communist etiquette might not have permitted a party leader to hold.

But this was not all. Being now a house owner but still without a job, he applied the labour of another six months, generated at the continued low cost of rice and beans, to the composition of a book which soon returned him to honour and prestige. Moreover, attracting a succession of bourgeois literary prizes, it also opened the door to more congenial sources of income. Persecution could not have paid more handsomely. Had he been seduced by offers of assistance, he would probably have ended the year as he began it—without either house or reputation, and his muscles atrophied.

There are many other cases of individual achievement, dramatizing the wealth-producing potential of the low cost of poverty whenever the muscle power extracted from a handful of rice is put to use rather than squandered in idle recrimination or self-commiseration. I am tempted to list them *en masse* for the benefit of those numerous angry young development statesmen trying to finance their windfall visions of progress by proudly casting a blackmailing right eye at the "exploiters" of Washington, while rivetting a humble solicitous left eye on the "redeemers" of Moscow. However, a single additional example will suffice: the array of unassociated efforts of a number of my Austrian middle-class friends laying the foundations of their subsequent affluence at the depth of economic dislocation and unemployment following World War II.

Their food rations were then as skimpy as they were cheap. But, having myself experienced similar scarcities as a schoolboy in Salzburg after the first world war, I knew that, though a dumpling with a little sauce, a slice of stone-hard black peasant bread three weeks old, or a bowl of lentil soup, are not much to look at, they can form both an adequate and an enjoyable meal.[1] The

---

[1] A low-cost "dumpling standard" is invariably considered as stunting, damaging, retarding the natural growth of healthy individuals. Yet, I still recall the delight we felt during my school days with a dinner consisting one day per week of three medium-sized potatoes with one thin slice of butter, or on other days, of one dumpling in thin beef broth. On excursion days into the mountains, we sustained ourselves with two or three slices of black peasant bread and a five-inch long compressed ribbon of sausage called *Landjäger*. Dishes rejected by more affluent societies such as left-over concoctions called *Beuscherl* or *Lingerl*, which cost perhaps a nickel to prepare, were our great favourites. They are still so popular with natives of Austria now living in richer environments that the *Blaue Donau*, a restaurant in upper Manhattan, was forced to increase their price from an orginal 25 cents to $1.50, since few of its customers cared for the more "substantial" conventional dishes such as Schnitzel, and in fact often travelled from places hundreds of miles away just to enjoy a lowly Beuscherl.

But the point I want to make concerns not the tastiness but the obvious medical wholesomeness of this kind of diet. It was during these years of "deprivation" that I won my only first prize in ski-racing, and that the generation of future Olympic champions was prepared. Nor did it interfere with intellectual work. During my college days in the early thirties, Hans Windischer, now Professor of Philosophy of the University of Innsbruck, and I met for daily study dinners consisting of a smoked herring and a loaf of bread between us, then walked lost in discussion along the Brenner-Pass road towards Italy until midnight. Yet, unlike most of the well-nourished students of today, who unload their knowledge the moment they have passed their examinations, strenuous peripatetics such as ourselves still remember much of what we learned 30 years ago as if we had picked it up yesterday.

black broth of the hardy race of ancient Spartans was nothing much to look at either. Yet, according to Plutarch, it, too, was so nourishing that "the elders did without the lumps of meat, leaving them for the children, while they themselves preferred plain soup." Moreover, it was so delicious that, on account of the broth, "one of the kings of Pontus was said to have bought a Spartan cook."[1]

I also knew that, far from having a debilitating effect, the involuntary frugality of my school-days gave us the leanness and strength for skiing over mountains, winning championships, swimming turbulent rivers, cycling the whole length of Europe, and climbing Alpine peaks which, at subsequent higher levels of nourishment, could be scaled only through feats of rockmanship by the fireside over a glass of brandy.[2] But what I did not know from my school-boy experience was the magnitude of the economic net product which a man working in isolation could realize over and above the cost of dumplings if he applied himself not to sport but to the accumulation of wealth.

This I only learned after the second world war when a number of friends from my native Austrian village, which I visited at annual intervals, decided to anticipate the example of Andreu Iglesias. Aware that it costs as much to subsist in idleness as at work, they began by diverting their underexercised labour power from analytical tavern oratory to the rebuilding of their houses. They added floors, or constructed new homes altogether. And when these were finished, they continued by adding garden adornments, guest quarters, swimming pools, week-end cottages, and a host of other luxuries such as they could never have acquired

---

1 Plutarch. *Life of Lycurgus*, 12.

2 To judge from another passage in Plutarch's Life of Lycurgus (17), this was also the reason inducing the Spartans to allow their boys only scanty meals: "in order that they may take into their own hands the fight against hunger, and so be forced into boldness and cunning. This is the main object of the sparse diet; a secondary one is to make them grow tall. For it contributes to height and stature when the vitality is not impeded and hindered by a mass of nourishment which forces it into thickness and width, but ascends of its own lightness, when the body grows freely and easily. The same thing seems also to conduce to beauty of forms; for lean and meagre habits yield more easily to the force of articulation whereas the gross and over-fed are so heavy as to resist it."

on the salaries earned in their conventional occupations.

Employing their then *socially* unemployable resources *personally,* they thus created each at a cost of perhaps $1,000 in dumpling-fed labour power and dumpling-produced raw materials, a total annual product of perhaps $10,000, or a net product of $9,000—a ratio which, if unsupported by significant amounts of capital, is surpassed only by artists at the height of their recognition. As a result, by the time they were reabsorbed in *socially* generated employment, and their table began to fill up again with *Wiener Schnitzel* in the place of dumplings, the use of their low-cost direct *labour* resources had surrounded them with an upper-class margin of affluence far beyond the reach of the high-cost *financial* resources available to the middle class anywhere else in the world.

And what happened in Austria, happened on an even more impressive scale all over Germany. However, since the bulk of the product, created during the first post-war years in seclusion, never left the privacy of the homes which it enriched, little of it registered on the radar screens of national income statisticians. As a result, when economists finally discovered the cumulative impact of this mass of unintegrated private activity, they were so stunned by the paradoxical side effects of total defeat that they called the now following second phase of post-war German reconstruction—fusing as it did isolated action back into the familiar pattern of complementary social co-operation, but materializing to all appearances out of thin air—a miracle.

Actually, as in the case of so many other puzzling occurrences, the whole mystery of the German miracle was simply that, left to itself as a result of the *laissez-faire* attitudes of Dr. Erhard, no one had looked when the stage was set up for its performance. What the German miracle really proved was therefore not so much what people can do in co-operation, but what man can do in isolation, alone, single-handedly—from Andreu Iglesias on a mountain top in tropical Puerto Rico to a brewer friend in my native village of Oberndorf near Salzburg.

Chapter Ten

THE FORCES DORMANT IN THE LAP
OF SOCIAL LABOUR

Out of difficulties grow miracles.
—LA BRUYERE

I F the preceding chapter tried to show what a solitary individual can do single-handedly, this is nothing compared to what even a few of us can do if we combine our productive power in integrated enterprise. One need only think of the achievement of the relatively small shock-troop units of competitive business organized by the capitalist bourgeois class in the century following the Industrial Revolution. As Marx, of all people writes so glowingly in the *Communist Manifesto,* of all places:

"The bourgeoisie, during its rule of scarce one hundred years, has created more massive and more colossal productive forces than have all preceding generations together. Subjection of nature's forces to man, machinery, application of chemistry to industry and agriculture, steam navigation, railways, electric telegraphs, clearing of whole continents for cultivation, canalization of rivers, whole populations conjured out of the ground—what earlier century had even a presentiment that such productive forces slumbered in the lap of social labour?"—And what a compliment to capitalism to come from the pen of Karl Marx!

Actually, earlier centuries were quite aware of what could be done by turning isolated individual into integrated social labour. The *vita communis* of humble Christian monks, which bequeathed to the world the awe-inspiring term "communism" along with its most successful operational scale, made fertile fields out of swamp lands and virgin forests, seeding valleys and hill tops with flourishing villages and the immortal learning and beauty of their monasteries. Medieval farm hands crisscrossed all Britain during the first enclosure movement within a few years after the black death with the most enduring network of sturdy stone fences ever created. Citizens of small Greek towns during the Peloponnesian war surrounded their territory with walls and double walls in a matter of weeks after learning of the hostile intentions of an enemy, while carrying on a full measure of their ordinary daily activities. Thebes, one of the most frequently destroyed communities of antiquity, rebuilt itself so fast each time it was sacked that as the geographer Pausanias notes, travellers expecting it in shambles were amazed to find it always modern, gleaming, and brand new—a tribute to how much can be created for how many by how few in how short a time.

But the most enduring monuments to the tremendous power stored in the lap of social labour of even a few are the countless instant "bootstrap" developments small communities were throughout history able to launch whenever a leader or a circumstance induced them to put their heart into it. When Peisitratus assumed power, Athens was an agglomeration of mud huts. By the time he departed from the scene, many of those architectural marvels were standing of which Pausanias wrote centuries later: "When they were new, they looked already ancient. Now that they are old, they still look new." And Athens was only one among many small communities transforming themselves in equally brief spurts of unaided social growth from drabness to the glory that was Greece—in a single generation.

Similarly, Augustus could summarize the achievement of a lifetime by saying: "I found Rome brick and leave it marble." True, Rome was the centre not of a small country but an empire. This is why she was so far behind in what the much envied capitals of her conquered provinces, unencumbered by the wastes of imperial scale, had achieved so much earlier. But even so, when Rome finally did get around to her own modernization, she managed it with local, not imperial, resources. And so did the numerous simultaneously emerging cities in the far away barbarian provinces of Germany, Britain, and Gaulle.

Continuing, one could go on citing examples from Antiquity through the Middle Ages right up to our own times. One could list the development feats of mercantilist duchies in France and cameralist principalities in Germany during the Renaissance. One could cite the Mennonite communities of early America. One could enumerate the spectacular contemporary development achievements of Iceland, Liechtenstein, the small Kibbutz villages of Israel, of Puerto Rico's widely publicized *Operation Bootstrap* of which its inspired leader, Luis Muñoz Marin, will one day be able to say with Augustus: "I found Puerto Rico shack and leave it stone."

And ending with an example from the other extreme of the publicity spectrum, one might cite a little known but hardly less dramatic development feat accomplished as recently as 1960 by Mr. Walter M. Hlady, an officer of the Canadian Indian Service. "Under conditions that could not have been worse," and at a cost (other than his own modest salary) "of only $12.64," Mr. Hlady managed to instill into the previously unorganized Churchill Band of Manitoba Indians such a drive for locally fuelled self-improvement ventures that their newly formed community, adapting its development to its native environment, began reaping the first fruit of a wholesomely diversified economy at the end of a period of barely six months.[1]

---

[1] I was informed of the Community Development Project of the *Churchill Band* of Indians of Churchill, Manitoba, Canada, by its originator, Mr. Walter M. Hlady, of the Canadian Indian Services, in the course of one of my lectures for the Canadian Institute of International Affairs. Furnishing me with an excellent illustration for my thesis, Mr. Hlady told the audience how, under his guidance, the until then wholly unorganized Churchill Band set out on its own self-improvement projects. Within the period of six months (between September 1959 and March 1960), it had established a hide-tanning industry yielding a revenue of $3,500.00 in the first half year; a dog-team service yielding as much as $20.00 per person in four hours of work; a birch bark handicraft industry; a Christmas tree business; and had set up a number of non-economic services of political, educational, recreational, and religious nature. In addition, telephone poles were cut and put into place during the same period for the improvement of communication.

As Mr. Hlady writes in *A Community Development Project Amongst The Churchill Band At Churchill, Manitoba* (Saskatoon, 1960), "conditions of employment, climate and other factors could not have been worse," when all this was achieved. The "results in a similar summer period would have been considerably more." But his most interesting observation for the benefit of the aid-requesting development statesmen of our time was this: "In direct outlay during this project, a total of only $12.64 was spent and $9.00 for beef brains is being recovered as women complete tanning hides and are paid

Thus, while collaboration—the fusion of individual into social power—is indeed essential for rapid progress, history proves that there is no need for any community, however small, to look for help from across its boundaries on the assumption that social labour of a larger community is more potent than the combined labour power of its own citizens. On the contrary! If the social power of large groups is to be rendered potent, it must itself first be broken up until the size of its working units is adjusted to the objectives to which it is to be applied. And since even the most comprehensive of personally meaningful objectives (leaving aside such questionable targets as the atomic conquest of time, space, and China) takes its measure from the small stature of man, the volume of social labour that can be used *economically* is by nature highly limited. For the law of diminishing returns applies of course also here.

This is why it is no coincidence that, as I am trying to show throughout this volume, the best framework for rapid progress was historically provided not by large powers relying on integration but by small communities proceeding in competition. Escaping the scatter effect of excessive scale, they alone were able to concentrate the gigantic power, generated by the fusion of social labour, on areas of such limited size that, in contrast to the sluggish growth of the giants, their spectacular achievements could often rise to their full height almost over night.

True, occasionally such rapid advance was experienced also in great powers. However, where this was the case, it was less due to the largeness of their sway than, as in the already cited example of the United States, to the groundwork laid in earlier periods by the tough elemental cells of small pioneer communities spreading in uninvolved polynuclear fashion across the entire continent, overcoming its hostile immensity by gradually splitting it up into convenient *CUV* units. And in the case of postwar

for their efforts. The remainder was spent on films." There was, of course, the additional expense of Mr. Hlady's own modest salary. But there was no outlay for the accommodation and entertainment of batteries of economic advisors, cocktail parties, Conferences on the problems of the Churchill Band, visits by senators, UN officials, dignitaries or members of the Oxford-Harvard Band. My only criticism for Mr. Hlady's work concerns his unforgivable failure to furnish a more detailed breakdown of the $12.64.

Germany, prepared by the unassociated efforts described in the preceding chapter, it was largely due to social life regrouping itself not in millstone unity but in the adaptive diversity of countless unassisted small businesses first springing back to life in the protective obscurity of small villages and small regions.

Which of course was nothing new; it was the oldfashioned way of early capitalism at the height of its flowering, when it achieved its ends not through government direction, mergers, or the large-scale co-operation of ponderous monopolists, but through the rivalries of a host of hot-headed small-scale competitors. And it is the new-fashioned way of Mao's communist China, building up, as it does, the nation through village-power rather than the other way round.

FROM MUD TO MARBLE IN A SINGLE GENERATION.

Chapter Eleven

PREVENTIVE COMMUNISM

*Nothing is so important at a dangerous crisis as that all should obey
the command of one unchallengeable chief.*
—PLUTARCH

Populus vult decipi, decipiatur.
—CARDINAL CARAFA

ACCEPTING then, as we must, that the power inherent in the
lap of social labour proved invariably amply adequate for
reaching in briefest time the most sophisticated development levels in even the smallest of past societies, the question
now is: Who was the magician releasing this potent store of
energy? Who provided the capital for triggering off the chain
reaction of progress?

There are only two ways by which countries can acquire their
necessary development capital: by accumulating it themselves, or
by borrowing it from those who have taken the trouble of doing
so. The historic way was always the first of the two alternatives.
Like Churchill's proudest achievement, this meant blood, and
toil, and sweat, and tears. It meant the initial storing of a portion
of the fruit of labour not as personal but as social wealth, taking
the form not of more butter but of more economic guns—irrigation canals, highways, public buildings, ships, factories. It meant
that part of the value produced by labour could not be returned
to it; that people had to work harder without at first getting commensurate individual rewards.

In other words, since capital is by definition frozen labour, or
product not consumed, the price of higher future standards of
consumption was always the temporary retention of the low standards of the past. As the Spartans built their empire through the
low cost of their famous black broth, and the Athenians the
Parthenon by continuing to eat porridge three times a day, so
mattress factories were financed by workers continuing to sleep
on straw, and cattle ranches, by farm hands continuing to prefer

dumplings to steak.

But this does still not answer the question as to the identity of the magician bringing all this about. Who was the sorcerer able to release the power bottled up in the lap of the social labour? Who the leader managing to persuade a society to assume the sacrifice of capital formation? Who the agent of progress capable of withholding from the workers the surplus value they were required to produce without offering them an instant share in the rising surplus product of their labour?

The obvious answer would seem to be: the profit-storing, and thus automatically capital-accumulating, private entrepreneur, deriving his command position from his ownership of the means of production. But, like the second stage of a rocket, the capitalist entrepreneur could soar to his vaunted heights of achievement only after having been carried aloft by the thrust of primary capital generated in the first stage. Being accelerator rather than originator, he could hardly have been responsible for triggering off a phase in economic growth that preceded his own appearance.

This leaves as the only alternative to the private accumulator, the public accumulator cf capital: the state. In pre-capitalist times, this was indeed the only agent powerful enough to impose on a society the burden of progress. Hence, the magician releasing the torrent of social labour was invariably a government of the most compelling authoritarian leadership which, moreover, was invariably backed by an equally compelling ideology able to make people bear their deprivations not only with resignation but with fervour.

This is the whole secret of the success of the Greek tyrants (a term not yet besmirched by the degradations of later autocrats), whose unlimited authority was backed by the oracular exhortations of Apollo. It is the secret of the productive power of the medieval Church, whose vast development programs were ideologically supported by the capital producing principle of *Ora et Labora,* pray and work, rather than work and be jolly. And it accounts for the nation-building activities of absolute princes and kings whose mercantilist capital formation was helped by the fun-spoiling Calvinist twin virtues of industry and frugality which caused everyone to work his head off and pile up goods, while at the same time abstaining from the latter-day Catholic joys of consumption, in the hope of thereby escaping the horrors of hell.

And in the more recent past, it accounts, in contrast to the undignified aid-dependent Yugoslav, Arabic, or Cuban experiments, for the proud unassisted development success of Soviet and Mao Communism which, for a time, was able to overcome even the retarding effect of their gigantism. In fact, similar to Calvinism earlier, communism seems nowadays the only ideology getting away with withholding from workers as much surplus value as capitalism was able to do at its worst: and with inflicting on the masses deprivations so severe that, imposed by anyone else, its own protagonists would call them outrageous reactionary practices. But it was precisely this shift from private to public exploitation rather than from exploitation to cornucopia that gave Russia the opiate of the first Sputnik orbiting our planet, and China the entrance ticket for joining the club of atomic hot-rodders and skin-heads.

In view of all this, is it nonsense to suggest as the best strategy for countries passing through their early development stages the frank adoption of systems into which their retardation is driving them anyway? That is, politically, to encourage them to fall openly back on an autocratic form of government, as former President Juan Bosch of the Dominican Republic did so courageously during his election campaign in 1969, instead of letting them continue to beat around the bush with the spiked necklace of democracy for the sake of a favourable notice in the *New York Times*?[1] And economically, would it not make more sense if they

[1] Former U.S. Assistant Secretary of State Harlan Cleveland suggested as much when he declared in the terms of Margot Preece of the *San Juan Star* during the installation ceremonies of Lawrence Wanlass as first President of the College of the Virgin Islands in 1964 "that legislatures should be 'outlawed' during the first independent years of new nations because the best men are drawn from the executive into politics." Soon afterwards, Kenya did precisely this, dissolving not the legislature but, what amounts to almost the same: the opposition. As the *New York Times* of November 11, 1964, writes: "This African country became a one-party state today. The change came as the Kenya African Democratic Party gave up its role as official Opposition in Parliament and joined the Government of Prime Minister Jomo Kenyatta. 'The Opposition is dissolved as of today,' said the party's leader, Ronald G. Ngala." As the report continues in a seeming but not real contradiction of terms, "his decision cleared the way for Kenya to become a republic."

were to immunize themselves against communism by swallowing a sizeable dose of it instead of being perpetually terrorized by the infection? Slay the ghost by bringing it to life?

In other words, instead of ineffectually trying to fend it off, should underdeveloped countries not unashamedly adopt "for the duration" an authoritarian system which, under the circumstances, might be called *preventive* or *development* communism?

Though many may be disturbed by such a suggestion, it is not quite so shocking as it seems. In the first place, there is already so much state socialism in today's overdeveloped "capitalist" great powers that, by comparison, development communism might actually appear as a case of conservative deviationism. This is why, as President Jaime Benitez of the University of Puerto Rico likes to recall, a number of leftist Latin American radicals were surprised when he asked them whether they planned to carry their socialist ideas as far as was done in the United States? They assured him they contemplated no such extremist measures for their own countries.

Secondly, though in its impact effect indistinguishable from *ideological* communism, the preventive vaccination with *development* communism would, by its very nature, create no more than a temporary rash on the skin. For in contrast to the former, which offers the restrictions of discipline and subordination in the interest of the greater glory of society as a way of life, as an end; development or preventive communism would offer them merely as a means for toughening the social fabric until it is strong enough to ensure the exercise of individual freedom to the citizen once the threshold of economic maturity is reached.

Similar to family communism, development communism would thus automatically be limited in *time* to the relatively brief period needed for society's leap into maturity. Like Marx's state, it would wither away with the fulfilment of its function. And it would be limited in *space* to the relatively small areas under the sway of its leaders. For, since development communism, if it is to be effective, must go hand in hand with the *CUV* approach, provision will have been made before-hand for the dissolution of the politically intoxicating and economically impoverishing unitarian large-area structures so beloved by ideological communists. What would therefore be left would be either a meshwork of chain-reaction preventing, unassociated, externally harmless, small development principalities providing each other with both checks (not cheques) and inspiration; or a loose federal system of self-sufficient, inward looking, small communities such as Robert Owen or John Stuart Mill envisioned as the corner stone of prosperous and peaceful co-existence.

Thirdly, unlike ideological communism, development communism would, of course, not preclude the setting-up of democratic institutions for *non*-economic concerns. There is no reason why functions such as education or justice should not remain subject to parliamentary processes, or why the freedom of the individual could not be safeguarded for the duration against excesses of government through the establishment of an independent and irremovable complaint authority patterned on the Scandinavian *Ombudsman*. Only in things economic would the authority of the head of government be near absolute, and even there only within the harmlessly small *CUV* area under his sway.

Finally, *development* communism might also yield a valuable fringe benefit. Obstructionist *ideological* communists such as the unemployed surplus graduates from the universities of Egypt or Ceylon could at last be silenced without arousing the wrath of their Russian, Cuban, or Chinese sponsors by making them for once the victims instead of the dispensers of their own prescriptions. They could be put under house arrest, as in Cairo. Or they could be sent for retooling to Peking, Moscow, or Havana, as was the method of the former head of state of Cambodia, His Royal Highness Prince Norodom Sihanouk Varnan. As the gifted cameralist development communist he was, he managed to gain approval for practically everything he did from the last persons one would have expected to give him support. He won the applause of the republicans by humbly retiring as King while retaining the infinitely more powerful positions of Commander-in-Chief, and Pontifex Maximus of Buddhism. He had the ear of the social revolutionaries by hanging on to as many royal titles before his name as Marshal Tito displays medals on his uniforms. And when seeking exile in Peking, he was given shelter by the very ideological communists whom his development communism tried to keep from power in his homeland.

On the other hand, this fringe benefit could barely matter. Since the hardship of generating capital at home instead of importing it requires the contribution of practically everybody in a not yet fully matured society, there would obviously be neither enough manpower, nor enough leisure, for filling the ranks of disgruntled obstructionists in the first place.

MANNING HOES INSTEAD OF TRACTORS SPEEDS UP DEVELOPMENT BY LEAVING NO TIME FOR MANNING ANTI-MAO GUNS.

Chapter Twelve

THE GIFT CONSUMPTION FUNCTION

*Thou shalt take no gift: for a gift blindeth them that have sight,
and perverteth the words of the righteous.*
—The Lord God

Rich gifts wax poor.
—Hamlet

THOUGH unaided capital formation through the imposition of a temporary rigorous, no-nonsense regime of preventive communism as pictured in the preceding pages should encounter little objection on the part of those anxious to avoid communism as a permanent feature in the life of grown-up nations, the idea is far from popular with a majority of contemporary nation builders. This is not because of the communist or authoritarian aspects of the proposition which some of them fancy anyway, but because of the idea of accumulating capital without outside aid. And there is something to it! For why should leaders have to strain their imagination, and the people their muscle and will power, when all the capital they need can be secured through such simple extractive devices as letting the youth wing of the ruling party smash the windows of American libraries, and then have the executive wing repair them by dressing them up in the baroque of democratic facades as eye-wash for the benefit of evangelists from the American Congress touring the globe with funds in search of recipients.

Borrowing or accepting capital as a gift is, of course, by far the simplest way of accumulating it. Indeed it is so effective that, under the heady influence of the blackmailing power of "neutralism," it is resorted to nowadays not only by unstable fledgling democracies but even by strong Moscow-backed Führer autocracies such as Cuba, Yugoslavia, Egypt, Algeria, or the Ghana of former Messiah Nkrumah. They all have shown that, instead of putting the tremendous development advantages of their authoritarianism to productive use at home, they would rather dissipate it by soliciting for their countries the corruption of a gift, instead of the blessings of an earned, standard of living.

Yet, they should long have discovered by now that financing progress with foreign capital achieves for a variety of reasons exactly the opposite of what proud nationalists should wish for their peoples. In the first place, it threatens their newly won political independence not only materially but also psychologically. For foreign investment "foreignizes'" a community even more than foreign occupation. Only domestically formed capital can avert this unwelcome consequence. But this cannot be accumulated in poor countries which are either prematurely exposed to democracy, or are governed by autocrats more interested in popular acclaim that assures their rule, than in the verdict of history which comes after they are dead. For what is needed in their case is the support of the majority. And the only way of gaining that support is of course not by promising the people blood and sweat and toil and tears, which *produce* capital, but transistors, cars, television sets, and sports stadia, which *consume* it. Since the need for continued majority support is particularly pressing in a democracy, it is not surprising that such a democratic stalwart as former President Johnson's Assistant Secretary of State, Harlan Cleveland, should have suggested that "legislatures should be 'outlawed' during the first years of new nations,"[1] a prescription to which one would have to add the constitutional provision that, where they have already been outlawed, the victorious autocrats should all be required to be practicing Calvinists.

Secondly, the ready availability of foreign-aid and gift capital causes the development process to *begin* with those wasteful overspills which make sense only at the affluent, or overfluent, terminal stage of nation building, when the dam is finished and the reservoir full, not when the construction workers are still busy mixing the concrete at the base. The reason for this fatal reversal of priorities is that the consumption function for gift and assistance income is radically different from that of earned income. Instead of encouraging economy and the judicious allocation of resources, it reflects the feeling of the beneficiaries that they have won a lottery which, in turn, stimulates their propen-

---

[1] For more detailed reference, see footnote on p. 68.

sity, not to save, but to blow every penny with voluptuous abandon.

One need but recall the squandermania of former President Maga of Dahomey who did the same thing as Renaissance princes, but with a difference. While the latter, drawing on income produced by already flourishing domestic economies, increased the wealth of their nations by indulging in the splash of palace building as the crowning achievement of unaided development, Maga succeeded in diminishing it by diverting externally procured assistance funds into his sumptuous residence to the tune of $3,000,000 long before his own country's economy was able to furnish the appropriate overspill.[1] Another example was brought to light by the first President of America's *Alliance for Progress,* Teodoro Moscoso, who told an audience of the type of rough going this famous assistance organization had in an unnamed country: "While economic advisors were advocating the purchase of heavy equipment with which to produce goods and materials to offset an unfavourable balance of payments, . . . the people of this particular country bought refrigerators instead, which produce ice for cocktails."[2] But even when externally procured assistance capital *is* spent on heavy equipment, it is even then almost invariably used for less rational purposes than would be the case with domestic capital. As Ceylon has shown, the first things it did with its foreign aid was to build a steel mill. Now that it has one, it has the prestige it fancied. But, as the papers report, the mill stands idle for most of the year since the country's entire supply can be produced in a matter of weeks. No wonder that, instead of creating employment, it provides the workers for the rest of the year with the leisure needed for preparing revolution against the very governments that thought of building up their pride.[3]

---

[1] TIME, November 8, 1963.

[2] The text of the quotation is not from Teodoro Moscoso but from the summary of a lecture by him contained in Professor Joseph K. Summers' column in the *San Juan Star* of March 25, 1965.

[3] Nearer at hand, I have myself been an example of the radically different and waste-inviting nature of the gift-consumption function. When a friend returned my cheque with which I thought I had bought his old car, and insisted that I accept it as a gift, I lost not a moment before squandering the

The Gift Consumption Function

Thirdly, because capital imported in too early a stage of development from outside an economy tends to *diminish* employment opportunities more than proportionately to those it creates; while domestic accumulation tends to *increase* them more than proportionately to those it eclipses (for the simple reason that the process of capital creation itself requires far more workers than the process of putting created capital to use); underdeveloped countries are forever confronted with the unpleasant fact that one of the first fruits of progress through foreign investment is the sudden emergence of an unemployment problem of dimensions which they are totally unequipped to resolve even *with* aid. And since a rising number of unemployed is a ready instrument of revolution not against mythical capitalists from abroad but against the government in power at home irrespective of whether it professes Maoism, Leninism, Marxism, or New-Leftism, the next consequence is that aid capital, meant to assist economic advance, must be diverted to military uses. For the only area with enough labour-absorptive capacity for defusing the revolutionary time bomb of unemployment is the army.

However, since the high cost of increasing the armed forces has a stunting effect on further development, the military employment of the unemployed does not extinguish the revolutionary sentiment once it has been awakened, but merely provides it with the professionalism, equipment, and leadership necessary for its fulfilment. As a result, as *doctores* Nkrumah, Obote, or Sukarno had to discover so painfully when it was too late: instead of adding a measure of safety to the spendthrift glory of liberation, governments yielding to the mephistophelian lure of creating wealth through the wand of aid capital, produced a side effect which tends to lead to the eventual overthrow not of poverty,

unexpected windfall funds in an act of wholly irrational Renaissance folly by resplendourizing the vehicle. Had I earned the sum, the embellishment of a car rendering excellent service in spite of a few scratches on the fenders would have been the last appetite I would have gratified as a rational economist.—Since no theorist, to my knowledge has ever given attention to the peculiar waste-inducing structure of the gift-consumption function, it might be worth an M.A. thesis for mathematically inclined students in economics to elaborate algebraically as well as diagrammatically its implications further, particularly in relation to development policy.

capitalism, or reaction, but of the leaders of the very revolution which put its trust in foreign investment as the easiest as well as the smartest way out of economic retardation.

And lastly, to mention the perhaps most undesirable side effect of foreign capital introduced too early for a country's development, it enables young nations to jump over the identity-shaping hardships of the vital intermediate stages of economic advance without even the benefit of speeding up the process. And since this is contrary to the laws of social biology, one may, paraphrasing Bernard Shaw, point out that all this can achieve is to cause them to slip from the dependence of infancy into the dependence of senility without the chance of ever passing through the phase of maturity. Is this worth the short-cut?

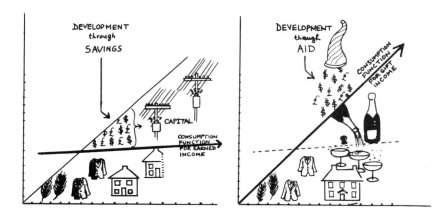

CONSUMPTION FUNCTIONS FOR EARNED AND GIFT INCOMES. THE FIRST SHOWS HOW FUNDS WITHHELD FROM CONSUMPTION TURN INTO CAPITAL; THE SECOND: HOW FUNDS ALLOCATED TO CAPITAL BUILDING ARE PREMATURELY DIVERTED INTO WASTEFUL CONSUMPTION.

Chapter Thirteen

PHASES OF DEVELOPMENT - I

The Village State

Multum in Parvo.

—PROVERB

A ssuming now that we have as leader a magician able to fire the imagination of the people; and assuming he has the governmental authority to make the labour force work on domestic capital formation, that is: with an eye not on the present but the future; for an increase in productivity but not yet in wages; for the creation of a healthy society but not yet for the improvement of the individual condition for which a healthy society is a prerequisite: what is the next step?

Our first task will be purely administrative. It is the division of our target country into a number of autonomous development districts of such small size that each can be managed with lucidity by people endowed not with genius, which is rare even in the advanced, but with ordinary horse sense, which abounds even in horses. Or to use the term introduced earlier, our first task is the division of the country into *CUV* regions which, in the beginning, need hardly be larger than monasteries, medieval manors, or modern collective farms. By definition, these can be developed by their local leaders without the requirement of either much graduate advice or close central supervision. This will help them avoid the wastes well described by Nikita Khrushchev when he complained that in gigantomania-stuck states such as the Soviet Union there are so many supervisors supervising supervisors that the objective of *super*vision is frequently all but lost from *vision*.

Our second task will be social. It is the establishment in our newly formed *CUV* districts of what I have called development communism. As already explained, this is a system which, unlike its ideological cousin, uses communism not as an end but as means, not as culmination but as ignition. It fades out as the motor catches on. The more retarded a region, the more complete will have to be its communism, just as the lower the starting point of a space rocket, the greater must be the initial thrust that ultimately frees it from dependence on the force hoisting it aloft, and enables it to proceed by its own momentum from then on.

In other words, a government preparing a retarded country for a life of affluent freedom, must impose the very restrictions we are most anxious to shed, in a measure directly proportionate to the degree of the country's retardation. In the case of extreme underdevelopment, this means the suspension at first of virtually all existing property relations. We may have to be housed in barracks, fed in common dining halls, and generally be subjected to disciplines associated not with free but controlled societies. Examples for this extreme form of "take-off" *vita communis* can be found even in our own day in the production communes of China, the Kibbutz communes of Israel, the monastic communes of the Catholic Church, the military communes of the Army, the sporting communes of rock climbers preparing an assault on Mount Everest. And there is no reason why—under the direction of an inspired leader, whom we have assumed to be indispensable in the early stages of growth—the soldiers of national development should accept the passing restrictions of the heroic phase of the struggle for a better life with less grace and gallantry than the soldiers of national defence.

Having prepared the ground through *administrative* division and *social* reorganization, we are now ready for the third and most important task. This is the organization of development at the *economic* level. While the two first objectives could be attained by simple act of law both instantaneously and simultaneously, the third task requires time. And everything requiring time must be broken down into a sequence, a succession of stages, a schedule of priorities, which will prove the more productive of desired results the more natural the order of their arrangement.

But what is the natural order of economic development in our manor-sized basic *CUV* commune? Should we start with the construction of highways? With the cars using them? With steel mills needed for both? With shelters for the workers necessary for all three?

If development is financed through outside assistance, any order is as good as any other, just as any method of managing a household, however wasteful, will prove successful if the housewife entrusted with it is married to a doting millionaire. But in the case of unassisted development, only a logical order is the natural order. And an order is logical only when every successive step is preceded by the completion of the step of which it is the immediate historic consequence. It is as with the human body. If it is to be well formed, it must during the nine months preceding birth pass in telescoped condensation through all historic phases of life preceding it: from sea creature to land creature; from fish to mammal to man. Skipping any of them would not speed up but stunt growth.

The natural, the logical, order is then the historical order. And historically, the first thing every society must do is to secure its food supply. This is hardly a problem considering that, from the frozen ocean worlds of the Eskimoes to the empty highlands of Tibet, there is no region on earth that does not provide the quantity and variety of food necessary for the survival of those originally living on it.

But mere survival is not progress. If a society wants to develop, it must aspire to more than the means of its bare subsistence. It must find ways for increasing its food productivity beyond the point up to which survival absorbs all available manpower. But this is hardly a problem either. For, all that is at first required for increasing primary productivity is: better organization of labour; wiser use of land; improved methods of cultivation; and a beginning measure of specialization. In this way, output per unit of labour can be increased without affecting the basic self-sufficiency of each of our manorsized *CUV* communes and, hence, without the need of resources from outside the local economy.[1]

[1] Examples of the superior self-financed agricultural efficiency of small *CUV* units adjusted to local talent both at communal and private levels of production are legion. As Joan Robinson, certainly no suspect of manorial medievalism, writes in her account of Chinese communes (*The Listener*, January 30, 1964): "In agriculture it is necessary to have a rather small unit

Once an increase in food productivity is achieved, the first brigades of social labour can be released from subsistence production for the accomplishment of the second step on the road to progress: the accumulation not yet of industrial but of our first agricultural capital. This takes the form of dams, irrigation canals, carts, field roads, fences, barns, as well as of warehouses and distribution centres for our henceforth jointly produced and owned subsistence commodities. And all we need for financing it, is the productive re-investment of the spare time we have gained as the first reward of our increased food productivity, instead of spending it immediately on an easier life, which would be more pleasurable. But it would leave us with no time to spare for capital building, and thus stop progress flat in its tracks at the moment of its inception.

Assisted now by new farm capital, our food productivity will at once experience a second boost. As a result, new brigades of

for controlling labour. People are spread out over the country. It is not like having them in the shop, in a factory, where one man can keep an eye on what is going on. The work is not regular, you have to take quick decisions: if it comes on to rain, should we go on cutting or should we stop? It is necessary therefore to have a diffusion of responsibility, and this means that a fairly small unit of control is needed. Secondly, the economic incentive, the relationship between the effort a man puts in and the result in his income, will be too much diluted if there are very large units; the economic incentive tells better in a small unit than in a large one."

This is even more borne out in the Soviet Union from where NANA reported in 1964 (exact date-reference lost), that, "while Kremlin Bureaucrats wrestle with the problem of how to grow more food on Russia's collective farms, millions of peasants are producing bumper crops on their tiny, privately-held plots . . . And year after year, the Russian peasants have produced proportionately more food on these private plots than on the huge collective farms, despite the absence of mechanical equipment and other forms of state aid . . . According to official Soviet figures, in 1961 the average potato yield on the collective farms was 7.1 tons per hectare. On the private plots, the potato yield was 11.6 tons . . . Private plots produced 45% of Soviet meat, 45.6% of the milk, 79% of the eggs, and 22% of the wool. Although the collective farms in Russia have more than 70% of the cattle in the Soviet Union, 74% of the pigs and 79% of the sheep, they were able to produce only 10% more meat than the private sector. Of the more than 200 million hectares under cultivation in Soviet Russia, less than 7 million hectares—about 3% of the total area—are worked as private plots," that is plots assigned to the private use of agricultural workers, as all land in the Soviet Union is state-owned.

manpower can be released for the third step in our historically logical development order. This is the construction of amenities which, for the first time, benefit no longer only society but its component parts, the citizens. Ushering in the gradual transition from social to individual purpose, from public to private property, from life in dormitories to life at home, the new cycle of activities thus provides us with our first individual residences, the first residential drainage and water systems, our first selective inns, shops, churches, and schools.[1]

In fact, grouped around the relaxed, uncostly charm of a market square alongside the as yet publicly owned communal warehouses and distribution centres, the structures added by this third step represent the attainment of our first comprehensive major development target: the self-sufficient rural *CUV* society; the prosperous manorial commune; the near-sovereign *village-state*. And we have accomplished it without outside economic aid of any kind—not in raw materials, considering that all we used in resources was what we found in our immediate neighbourhood; not in food, considering that our first advance took the form of an increase in our own food productivity; nor in funds, considering that every addition to our wealth has so far been financed by the use of spare labour released by each of the

---

[1] The speed with which the transition from social to individual purposes, from life in dormitories to life at home, is achieved is again well demonstrated by Joan Robinson writing on the fate of the collective canteens of Chinese communes (*op. cit.*): "Also the canteens have gone out of fashion: I did not find any commune where they were now running a canteen except for convenience in the rush season. Under the present system the income of a family depends on their earnings for work, and they do their cooking at home in the ordinary way. I do not regard this as a breakdown; I regard it as common sense." It also illustrates the *self*-liquidating nature of communist modes of life in *small* communities, which inexorably wither away in proportion as the targets of "development communism" are accomplished.

2 What happens when countries jump over the vital village-state phase in their development, leaving vast agricultural lands underutilized by their prior failure to tie their population down in the reinforcing meshwork of highly self-sufficient rural communities, is shown in the disastrous imbalance of urban growth. As TIME (February 7, 1964) reports of "Latin America's 220 million people, 45% now live in cities, and the percentage is rising as more and more people seek to escape the unemployment and near starvation of the countryside." Under normal conditions of development, the Physiocrats'

successive waves of higher efficiency following in the wake of every successful increase in our food productivity.

In other words, by means of direct-labour finance in the place of complicated, indirect, imported-capital finance, our development has so far cost us nothing. This is true even if we measure the result in terms not of foreign capital but of domestic sacrifice. For the same amount of labour that previously yielded us less now yields us more—partly through better organization, which costs nothing; partly through primary capital created through better organization, which again costs nothing except in terms of the only currency that everyone has at his disposal: time.

Nor is this just another case of ivory-tower economics or manorial romanticism. Its down-to-earth realism could not have been borne out better than by the eye witness account in *The Listener* (January 30, 1964) of the tough, rough, great Joan Robinson of Cambridge, who could hardly be accused of either. Describing the unaided agricultural capital formation on a Chinese commune through labour released (in her example) not by increased food productivity but, what amounts to the same thing, the seasonal ebbing of farming activities, the grand old lady of Economics is very emphatic in making the point that all this was achieved without the expense of a penny. For labour, the main factor behind all primary capital formation, "cost nothing because it is in the slack season when there is no other work to do," and

produit net of the land nourishes the trading classes of the city. It is not the other way round: the mercantile profits of the city, nourishing cultivators of the land. If this order is reversed, the unimaginatively starving countryside does not improve itself by moving into the city, but merely drags the city down to its own starvation level by turning, in the words of TIME, a bean field at the edge of Columbia's port city of Barranquilla "into a shantytown of crude huts housing 2,500 people. Lima's slums are growing ten times faster than the city itself; 450,000 live in slums today, compared with 120,000 in 1957 . . . Brazilian cities must build one new house or apartment every two minutes to keep up with the growth rate . . . and even Sao Paulo's amazing building boom is good for only one every ten minutes." Venezuela's answer, which TIME thinks is "striking closer to the heart of the problem," is "to develop brand-new industrial complexes away from the overburdened major cities." But the result of this will of course be not less but more urban cancer, by giving the rural population, instead of anchoring it at last in wholesome village communities on the land, an added incentive to engulf the city, contributing to the decay of both.

workers must of course be sustained just the same. In this manner, the communes "enrich themselves permanently by increasing the fertility and convenience of their land, which they are going to work in the future. There one can see with the naked eye how the organization of the communes helps create wealth for themselves."

The same goes of course also for "anti-communist" communes such as the South Viet Nam village of Hoaimy whose unexpected release of social energy seems, accoding to TIME (May 1, 1964), to have left a trail of observers in "stunned" awe. What happened was that "suddenly and, as far as anyone can tell, on their own initiative, 10,000 villagers turned out for 27 straight days," and built unassistedly, voluntarily and without payment by means of hoes and baskets a ten-mile long wall 10ft. high, 20ft. wide at the base, and 4ft. wide at the top. Then they surrounded its entire length with a moat which "was filled with water lifted from the river by paddle-wheel scoop."

Using apparently spectacles from the Tales of Hoffman instead of Joan Robinson's "naked eye," the correspondent of TIME thought there was "something mysterious and mystical about the great wall of Hoaimy." And his editors felt that "the answers are not simple and cannot be precise." Yet in the next sentence they provide themselves an answer both simple and precise. "Hoaimy," they explain, "is a singularly cohesive community;" which makes it an ideal operational *CUV* unit capable of releasing instant labour power. And it is directed by Truong, "an exceptionally good district chief who lived and worked alongside the villagers;" which provided it with the ideal manorial development lord capable of assigning the available excess labour power to the capital building projects the situation demanded.

This is all there is to the marvel and mystery of Hoaimy's unassisted achievement in the midst of the non-achieving and lavishly assisted non-marvels of the rest of Viet Nam. What the nation-state could not accomplish *with* aid, the village-state completed *without*.

Chapter Fourteen

PHASES OF DEVELOPMENT - II

The City-State

*I never learned how to tune a harp or play
the lute; but I know how to raise a small
and inconsiderable city to glory and greatness.*

—THEMISTOCLES

HOWEVER, happy as the self-sufficient, and materially prosperous village-state may be, full economic development requires the scaling of greater heights. In addition to rural affluence, we want urban amenities. We want libraries and hostelries; market places and universities, theatres and cafés; hospitals and cathedrals; stone pavements and marble fountains; architecture and style. And we want workshops and factories, the social and industrial capital which becomes necessary in addition to a larger supply of our original agricultural capital, if we are to turn our now hightened ambitions into reality. But since no village-state disposes singly over a population numerous enough to provide the specialization needed for the fulfilment of these higher aspirations, our next major target is the pooling of their resources through the federal integration of several of the now mature manorial communes into a larger *CUV* entity—the city-state.

As is the case with every integration, the resulting transfer of self-sufficiency from a number of smaller to a single larger unit will somewhat diminish the previous self-sufficiency of now component parts. Moreover, turning an independent local non-trading into an interdependent regional trading community, we must incur the cost of extra equipment, transport arteries, and bureaucrats needed for handling our scale-enlarged new tasks of exchange and distribution. However, since the higher degree of specialization made possible by regional integration furnishes at the same time the basis for a new and more than proportionate increase in productivity, it provides us automatically also with the additional labour brigades required for the execution of the main task now ahead of us—the building of the city as well as the establishment of its attendant administrative, cultural, manufacturing, and trading institutions.

The ability to release new waves of surplus labour at the culminated village level is thus the *general* reason explaining why the fulfilment of the greatly extended aspirations of the city-state requires once again as little in outside assistance as was necessary for the realization of the more modest aspirations of the earlier village-states. But there are also a number of *special* reasons for this.

1. First of all, we must remember that we are integrating the constituent village communities after, not before, they have reached a high plateau of maturity and prosperity in their own right. Their new interdependence will therefore merely entail an extension of their already existing rural activities rather than imply a costly change in direction and elemental structure; a simple strengthening of organs rather than a complicated transformation of functions. The limited scope of integration will therefore reduce the previous 100 per cent self-sufficiency of the villages by no more than perhaps 10 per cent. For the number of *new* intra-regional traffic arteries and other facilities needed for both feeding the emerging city and fusing it economically with its hinterland is, by nature, so small that it will barely tax the joint resources of constituent communities already basking in a high degree of individual affluence.

Moreover, the minimal loss of rural self-sufficiency will not only keep down the cost of integration but offer the inestimable concomitant advantage of enabling the new state to preserve the wholesome dualism of contrasting forms of country and city life. For to the extent that the villages are able to retain a substantial measure of autarchy, they are automatically provided with the only economically effective weapon against the otherwise inescapable erosion of their identity and the migration of their inhabitants into the desolate uniformity of suburbs—a cancerous growth which is neither country nor city and, in Aristotle's terms, may cause a society at length "to attain such a degree of unity as to be no longer a state—since the nature of a state is to be a plurality." (Politica, II, 2).

2. Aside from the high degree of affluent rural self-sufficiency, a second main reason for the possibility of the unaided achievement of the next phase of development lies in the low cost of the *type* of city which we are telescoping out of its parental conglomerate of village-states. For unlike the vastness of modern political associations, the limitation of the city-state in both its national and urban territory enables it to save the three most sterile as well as most crushing *economic* wastes of our time: a) the stupendous costs nowadays incurred in urban commuting, which fall away if cities are again built as dense, compact, traffic-saving centres of pedestrian dimensions: b) the equally stupendous costs of long-distance haulage, which fall away if a small society adjusts its developmental appetites to what can be produced with the manpower and material resources available within the narrow confines of its own neighbourhood; and c) the overspill cost of a highly trained technocracy and bureaucracy of outside advisors and domestic administrators which are as indispensable as they are useless in nations that have outgrown the dimensions of "naked-eye" translucency, but can be done without in the unencumbered *CUV* proportions of an unaffiliated city-state.

The ability to save the last-named waste represents not the least of the economies possible in a small community. To appreciate this, we need but consider the astronomical cost of a modern techno-bureaucracy resulting from the double-drag of the high remuneration it commands because of its long preparation, and the stifling red-tape effect it exerts because of the notorious inverse relationship between the need for its services and the efficiency of its performance. For as Northcote Parkinson has so brilliantly shown, the less a bureaucrat accomplishes, the longer must the citizen sit at his feet. And the more he advises on the process of development, the larger becomes the army of additional bureaucrats who must be called in to sort out the tapes of the consultants (whom the late Howard Gossage used to define as persons who borrow your watch and then tell you what time it is. And, as someone added, then keep your watch).

The saving of the wastes of bureaucracy has, moreover, the advantage of furnishing us with the self-generating domestic talent pool from which we can in due course draw the physicians, teachers, artists, fashion designers, entertainers, architects, lawyers, goldsmiths, and all the others needed for filling the full range of urban occupations which begin to spring into existence when physical construction and capital formation have reached the point at which they can be reduced to the requirements of mere maintenance. This is when the resource-consuming economies of growth can give way to the dividend-yielding economics of form; and when the contraction of employment coming with the completion of expansion no longer heralds so much the dreaded advent of the stationary state as the emergence of the different *type* of employment that characterizes the arrival of civilization.

3. Finally, there is a third important cause that enables the city-state to develop to its fullness without outside assistance. This is the temporary retention of the system of development communism. As we have seen, this has historically been achieved in the villages under the disciplined leadership of what earlier periods would have called the Lord of the Manor, but our militarist age is more likely to refer to as District Chief or Development Commissar. And the agent applying it in the nascent city-state would previously have been known by the more humble title of Prince, but in our republican environment is more sweepingly referred to as President-for-Life, Benefactor, Liberator, Generalissimo, or Redeemer.

The reason why development communism continues to remain an essential factor in the self-help financing of progress during the early stages of the city-state is that it spares us also by far the costliest of *political* wastes (always provided that our development principality is prevented from following the example of ancient Rome by expanding beyond the lucidity of its original *CUV* proportions): This is the waste of premature democracy.

To appreciate this, we need but envisage the expenditure in time, money, and liquor incurred in consultation, deliberation, reflection, committee dissipation, debating, campaigning, and what not. As democracy itself, practices of this nature are cherished as well as inspiring luxuries that can not only be afforded once the plateau of maturity has been reached; they are then even essential in engaging the otherwise explosive volume of civic energy released with the attainment of full material development. But for retarded societies in the midst of their struggle for rapid advance, such practices of maturity make about as much sense, and are as ruinous, as parliamentary deliberations are for armies in the midst of battle. For what both need at that juncture is not consultation but action; not hesitation but determination; not consensus but leadership; not approval but vision; not fear of error but the courage of moving ahead even at the risk of being wrong. For an error committed fast, can also fast be corrected. And this is preferable to the safeguards of committee compromise which, instead of focussing responsibility, socializes it; and instead of insuring against error, often compounds it by making it unanimous, adding to the cost of delay, the cost of being wrong for a long time to come.

There seems thus no reason why a modern city-state of *CUV* proportions should not be able to reach the most sophisticated levels of Florentine development unaided[1] as long as it is willing to apply the afore-sketched history-tested simple-guide-lines: 1. Integrate village communities only when they have attained enough self-sufficiency and rural affluence to produce the over-spill necessary for supporting an urban society of their own making. 2. Save the *economic* wastes of integration (a) by combating urban sprawl through the construction of compact cities preserving a high degree of pedestrian proportions; and (b) by

[1] As a random example illustrating the minuscule dimensions of multitudes of city states able to reach unassisted development levels that are still the delight and envy of modern man, let me quote from a nostalgic travelogue by Alfred Delig in the *Industrie Kurier* of March 5, 1964: "Until the threshold of the 19th century, that is until 1806, Upper Suabia consisted of dozens of ecclesiastical and secular principalities and an untold number of free cities of the realm, all anxious to demonstrate their political independence through great architectural achievements. This explains the abundance of magnificent castles and palaces, world famous churches and monasteries, and last but not least well preserved cityscapes. Surrounded by high walls and turrets, they enshrine marvels of architecture, hallowed cathedrals, precious city-halls, and fresco-adorned patrician palaces often hidden in the midst of a dense meshwork of intertwined streets. Little cities with great history . . ."—And Upper Suabia, of which all this forms part, is itself merely a part of a small region, Suabia, which in turn is only a part of a small state, Wurtemberg.

keeping the interdependence between city and country on the one hand, and among the villages on the other, at an indispensible minimum. 3. Save the *political* wastes through the temporary retention of authoritarian development communism or, if you prefer a more historic name, of cameralist absolutism or benevolent despotism, in the place of a premature democracy which stresses experience in debate before having acquired experience in action.

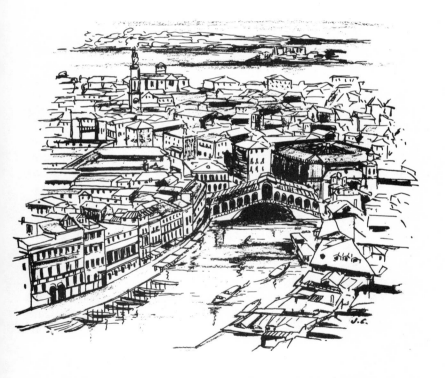

THE LOW-COST LUXURY OF URBAN CONTRACTION.

Chapter Fifteen

CULMINATION:
THE TRANSLUCENT SOCIETY

*The best limit to the population of
a state is the largest number which
can be taken in at a single view.*
—ARISTOTLE
Au volant, la vue est la vie.
—FRENCH CAR STICKER

Now, as far as I am concerned, development could just as well stop when it has reached the culminating level of the city-state.
We now have practically everything a mature community might desire. The village-state has given us all we could wish in food, shelter, and clothing. And the city-state has added to it leisure, elegance, grace, and style. We have united a hundred or so neatly built, closely packed, small rural communities, leaving the forests and fields surrounding them swept clean, interlaced with a network of lanes and limpid streams, and crossed here and there by a tree-lined highway accommodating the leisurely traffic into town. And in the midst of it all, we have created our crowning citadel: a buzzing dense little metropolis, its gleaming spires looking down into the swarming pedestrian amplitude of marbled squares, colonnaded enclosures, hidden patios, dreamy fountains, sidewalk, cafés, bridges, factories, and balconied shady streets converging, free of traffic gluts, like the lines of an intricate spider's web, on the resplendent central plaza of our commonwealth.[1]
And, on top of it, we have achieved something else. Now that

[1] Hearing such talk, economist friends invariably call me a romantic. Do they realize the high profitability of romanticism? The income derived by Venice from its gondolas? By Conrad Hilton from the birds of paradise in his lobbies? By Disneyland from fairy tales? By astronauts circling the moon? For a rationalist, a life ending in the bankruptcy of death, is economically a wasted expenditure, a loss proposition to begin with. Only a romantic can

our city-state has reached maturity, we can dispense with the system of authoritarian development communism that has helped us bring it about. For at last we can afford what previously would have been a wealth and time-consuming luxury. Politically, we can afford freedom and democracy because now we have time. And economically, we can afford the variety-enriching duplications, and "wastes" of competitive free-enterprise because now we have wealth. In other words, with the city-state fully matured, the stage is set for simultaneously reducing both the political and the economic machinery of government, and for handing the bulk of the economy over to individual entrepreneurs.

This is exactly as it happened throughout history. Whenever a society had completed the task of laying the communal foundation of its economy, the caterpillar of control transformed itself into the butterfly of freedom. Hence the (not at all contradictory) seeming paradox of uninhibited *laissez-faire* systems following invariably in the footsteps of the most autocratic development and control systems. In the 19th Century, they followed the state socialism of cameralism and mercantilism. In our own time, in the smaller countries affected by it, they will follow communism. And they will follow it not only in its developmental but even in its ideological variety.

True, this contradicts Nikita Khrushchev's sepulchral prediction prior to his own political demise that communism will bury capitalism. Actually, he was quite right. It *will* bury it for two reasons. First, as I have tried to show, communism is the only system that can speedily and unassistedly solve our time's development problems. And secondly, the declining overdeveloped large capitalist nations of the world—decaying not because they are capitalist but because they have outgrown self-manageable *CUV* dimensions—are themselves increasingly becoming as dependent on socialized government direction as were until now only the emerging underdeveloped countries of both the 18th and 20th centuries. Witness the helplessnes of Rolls Royce.

make sense of it, as only a romantic can see sense in a mankind wastefully split in free-enterprise fashion into a mass of independent small nations living in amiable rivalry, rather than submitting to the monopolistic unistructure of a Tower of Babel saving in overhead costs, and rationally communicating in the unispeak medium of Pidgin English.

What Khrushchev seemed to have overlooked however is that —to the extent that the primary task of all forms of communism is to restore, through the application of a curative *CUV* pattern, economic vigour to societies tottering because of either under or overdevelopment—communism will eventually come into the same position, once it has reached its target, which Marx predicted for the state. It will lose its function. It will become superfluous. Hence, like the mercantilist control system before it, it will wither away. That this is not idle speculation can be seen from the fact that the eminent Soviet economist Esvey Liberman has already begun calling for a return to greater reliance on private initiative and other typically *laissez-faire* incentives from his chair at the University not of Detroit but of Kharkov; from the stronghold not of capitalism but the very heartland of communism. And characteristically, he could risk doing so without any apparent fear of being branded a capitalist grave digger, as would have been his fatal lot a few years earlier, when communist development was not yet sufficiently advanced.[1]

But now that it is, it is no longer either surprising or revolutionary for a theorist such as Professor Liberman to arise, and perform the same ideological ice-breaking function in communist Russia as was performed 200 years earlier in mercantilist England by Sir James Steuart, whose pioneer doctrine of the self-equilibrating mechanism of demand and supply amounted likewise to a call for reducing the then still all-pervasive body of government controls.

True—like his current Soviet successor, Steuart continued to acknowledge the ultimate precedence of state over private interests, and is therefore not unjustly called "the last mercantilist" rather than "the first capitalist". But with the age of nation building drawing to a close and, as a result, with the need

[1] See the excellent account on Liberman and the gradual withering of Soviet communism in *Time*, February 12, 1965. It also shows the relationship between a return to free-enterprise methods and reduced national size on the one hand, and economic advance on the other by pointing to the fact that Russia has been preceded in the toning down of centralized state controls by her smaller (and hence not unreasonably more advanced) satellites, by years, as for example by Czechoslovakia under the influence of Professor Otis.

for continued individual subordination to social design rapidly dwindling, Steuart had hardly published his already mellowed form of mercantilism in *Principles of Political Economy* (1767), when Adam Smith appeared on the scene with his *Wealth of Nations* (1776). And Smith condemned even mellowed government controls as interfering with the processes of nature, and as extraneous to the architecture of an economy that' had reached maturity. As the scaffolding of wood must come down from cathedrals which it may have taken centuries to build in stone, so Smith showed that the scaffolding of government controls must be dismantled when the edifice of the nation stands completed, however hallowed their antiquity, and however entrenched the busy construction interests, which had become accustomed to making their living on them.

It is thus quite reasonable that communism should perform the last rites for the corpse of capitalism in times of prematurity and decay. But, to judge by both the logic of development and historic precedent, is it less reasonable to expect that capitalist free enterprise in the small-scale Smithian sense will in due course return the kindly gesture, and bury the corpse of communism with the advent of social maturity, which communism itself is so suicidally committed to bringing about through the very process of succeeding? The Kremlin's generous grave digging offer rests therefore on a basis of strict reciprocity. For as Smith followed Steuart in 18th century England, an Adamov Smithovich is likely to arise on the heels of Esvei Liberman in contemporary Russia —always provided, of course, that the regionalization trend, begun with Khrushchev's economic division of the immense Soviet Union into a meshwork of districts more in line with CUV proportions, does not yield to centralized gigantomania once more under the successors who deposed him.

However, similar to man's self-reliant freedom in his prime, free political and economic systems can maintain their vigour only in periods of maturity. Does this mean democracy and free enterprise will always be short-lived? By no means. For though maturity cannot be perpetuated in the human body at all, it can be preserved in the body politic indefinitely. All that is needed is to preserve the human scale embodied in unimpaired CUV proportions. In other words, once social maturity is reached, the way of saving its political and economic freedoms from grave-digging kremlins is not by fostering further growth, but by ultimately stopping it altogether. If this cannot be achieved, the result will always be overgrowth and collapse.

And it is because of the danger of overgrowth setting in when the *natural* mission of growth has been accomplished, that I started this chapter by suggesting that, as far as I was concerned, development might just as well come to a halt when it has reached culmination in the unharrassed, uninvolved, cancer-resisting small-cell system of the largely pedestrian city-state. This would give man the benefits not only of the Affluent but, what is more important, the Translucent Society whose limited scale makes problems soluble by making them visible to the naked eye.

NOT STATE, NOT NATION, NOT MACHINE—*MAN* IS THE
MEASURE OF ALL THINGS.

Chapter Sixteen

PHASES OF DEVELOPMENT - III

The Nation-State

"Magna civitas, magna solitudo"
—LATIN PROVERB

IN spite of my Aristotelian and Augustinian faith in the Translucent Society, and my conviction that man would hence best be served if material growth were to come to an end once the culminating pinnacle of the city-state is achieved, I am aware that this is contrary to the unity-struck and expansion-drugged temper of our time. And it may even be contrary to the design of nature itself which, in its periodic need to renew itself, gets rid of existing systems by the very process we try to avert: by ageing them. And its way of ageing them is paradoxically by releasing once again the dammed-up growth energies of their component cells by weakening the walls created for containing their size within the limits of their function-determined form.[1] For

[1] One of nature's most effective ways of extermination is by stimulating overgrowth—making things too large for their purpose. Modern gardeners make use of this when they kill weed no longer by laboriously tearing it out but by cunningly injecting a growth serum through which the weed conveniently kills itself by imperialistically expanding beyond its function-determined optimum form. On the other hand, nature's way of preserving things while at the same time increasing the base of life, is to proceed in the opposite direction: instead of stimulating growth, it contains it; instead of cancerously expanding form, it duplicates it. Julian Huxley, in his lecture on "Biological Improvement", (*The Listener*, November 1, 1951), has called this process "adaptive radiation," and shown how, by branching off into species and subspecies, more life is sustained by a wider range of non-competitive food sources than would be possible if a single species would overexpand for lack of differentiation. In the latter case, a myriad of food resources not adapted to the particular requirements of the expanding species

nature knows that renewed growth in the mature is not the same as in the young. It nudges them not to higher levels, but over the top; not to greater maturity, which is logically inconceivable, but into senility which does not become more hopeful simply for

would go to waste, with the result that life would be that much less abundant. Had all of us become steak-eating Americans or maccaroni-eating Italians, the food resources of the arctic or the highlands of Tibet would have remained unutilized. By adaptively branching off into Eskimoes and Tibetans, prairie people and mountain dwellers, that many more of us can make a living on that much greater a variety of nourishing substances.

It is because of nature's method of progressing through adaptive radiation rather than unification that dangers must inevitably arise if the process of social merger is carried to the point where the variety-insuring tribal dimensions of small communities, village and city states, begin to give way to the unadaptive inflexibility of massive nation and world states. The same situation may then confront the human race that threatens the abundance of wildlife in Tanganyika where "civilizing" man, not content with confining integregation to his own kind, tries to subject also the animal kingdom to the fatal modern trend of function-disrupting unification. Favouring the introduction of homogenous large populations of a single high-yield species (domestic cattle) over the still existing fascinating variety of countless small ones, he runs the risk of narrowing ultimately the subsistence base not only for the country's animals but also for himself. For just as a number of smaller firms have been shown to be more productive as separate entities than as parts of a combination (see, for example Monograph No. 1e of the Temporary National Economic Committee, *Relative Efficiency of Large, Medium-sized, and Small Business);* or as the great number of rival languages of limited reach have created a richer treasure of combined literature than would have been possible in a single language whose accessibility to all would have persuaded most that everything has already been said; so has it been shown by experiments "that various species of wild game produce three to seven times as much meat per square mile of grazing land as domestic cattle—an important factor in deciding the most economic use of land."

In other words, as Paul Brook writes in *The Golden Plains of Tanganyika (Horizon,* Vol. VIII, No. 1), just as in human environment: "Here variety is not merely the spice but the condition of life." A country like this, "when undisturbed, can support large numbers of wild animals because over aeons of time each species has evolved in such a way as to find its own ecological niche. Whereas in a herd of cattle each cow is competing with its neighbour for the same blade of grass, in a mixed herd of wild animals the different species utilize the various grasses, shrubs, and trees which grow together in the same area. As the wellknown ecologist Lee M. Talbot has written: 'Food preferences of these wild unregulates are to a large degree complementary to each other and the plant species preferred are often those unpalatable to domestic lifestock."

being called a second infancy. But while nature knows all this, our statesmen and their economists seem to dismiss it as an out-dated case of obsolete physiocracy.

So we must carry on and, for better or for worse, push the process of economic growth an uneasy step further by gathering up a number of healthy city-states into the vastly extended entity of the nation-state.

One of the few things that can be said for the nation-state is that, at this juncture, we can at least afford it. So even this last extension of development can be financed without a penny of outside aid. And the reason for this is the same that has accounted for the unassisted creation of the city-state out of village-states: we are fusing the regional economies not *in order* to develop them but *after* they have already reached a full measure of affluent maturity in their own right. In contrast to prematurely enlarged economies, very little need therefore be built up from scratch. In fact all that must now be done is to add the material and institutional superstructure necessary for the integration rather than for the development of the new nation-state.

This is why the cost of continued expansion will once again lie well within our resources, in spite of the fact that we have at last reached the point where we need—but backed by the combined wealth of our regional city-state economies are also for the first time able to supply—those costly fetishes that make the advertisements of modern progress so dazzling: the far-flung superhighways, long-distance railroads, cars, trucks, jumbo-jets, *Concordes,* as well as the power plants, steel mills, and all the rest of the equipment which indeed, no city-state could ever have afforded singly. Nor, however, would any city-state ever have needed them nor, for that matter, any ordinary citizen, whose ambition in pursuit of happiness former President Johnson has, even in the case of satiated America, identified as "not too large. They boil down to food, shelter, and clothing."[1] But these, also a village-state is capable of furnishing in amplitude.

The bargain a nation-state can offer is thus barely worth it. All it can do is to add to our social rather than personal consumer goods. It can overwhelm us with remedial rather than happiness

[1] As reported in *Time,* May, 1964.

commodities; with necessities to meet the difficulties of irrationally existing on an extended scale, which increase the *cost* of living, rather than with luxuries that might raise our *standard* of living, and increase our leisure for enjoying it. In short, it promises us the great *society* instead of the greatness of *man*—which can hardly be said to be a bargain.[1]

However, the real problem of the nation-state is of a different kind. Its organization constitutes territorially the first step on the road towards those magnitudes that lie beyond manageable *CUV* proportions. Being larger in size than our unaided natural vision can encompass, it opens the gate to the danger of being ultimately devoured by the insurveyability of its own dimensions. Actually, this is what is already happening in nation-states such as Germany, Britain, Italy, France, or the United States. After a lively period of seemingly indestructible *laissez-faire* existence, the self-centred vigour of their economies seems spent. As a result, they find themselves today in the same position they had occupied 150 years earlier, when they were still largely underdeveloped. Sliding down the other side of the mountain, and approaching in accelerating tempo Khrushchev's famous burial grounds, they are, as they were then, once again dependent on a heavy measure of government control.

Yet, the trend towards increasing government dependence is not necessarily doomed to run its full course. It can be avoided if the nation-state is willing to retain, or able to restore, the inestimable *CUV* advantages of its original city-state economies, by preserving so much of their regional self-sufficiency that the nation-state would actually, from an economic point of view, hardly be needed.[2] To this end, it would have to resist the temp-

[1] For an idea of the cost to the individual citizen of membership in great societies see my table in *The Aspirin Standard (Business Quarterly,* Summer 1956).

[2] The restoration of *CUV* proportions was admittedly one of the main targets of the two economic divisions of the Soviet Union: in 1957 into 105, and in 1961 into 17, highly autonomous economic regions. The maximum regional populations under the second division ranged from 8 to 14 million, with the exception of a central district of 25 million. This put an end to the previous communist policy ideal of organizing the Soviet Union as *One Country, One Factory,* which, after 40 years of experimentation, was at last discarded as Stalinist gigantomania. Aside from the hope of thereby

tation of extending its sway into every phase of life. Rather, it would have to keep its scale-dominated "national" involvements down to an irreducible minimum. Instead of integrating the economy as a whole, it would have to weave together only those of its strands needed for servicing it, such as telephone or inter-regional transportation, dining and sleeping car facilities. In other words, its unity would have to resemble the unity of an apartment house which, likewise, intergrates not the individual flats of its tenants, but only the basic services needed for the maintenance of their common structure, such as electricity, garbage disposal, heating, water, lobby, doorman, and elevator facilities.

Similarly, interregional trade would have to be confined to those operations that may still confer upon the citizen a positive gain over the local abundance of the city-state. It may thus be encouraged where it helps in the distribution throughout the nation of the handful of delicacies and luxuries which, by their nature, can be produced only in its separate regions. But it should not be encouraged to the point where the medium becomes the message by turning into its own purpose and beginning to swamp the citizen with a plethora of remedial commodities which, such as commuter and travelling equipment, are not wanted but needed for spanning distances which excessive integration has transformed from adventure into a chore.

If these limiting principles are observed, then also the *tools* of national integration and trade can be held to a minimum. Taking their scale from the size of the political body they serve, instru-

restoring greater administrative translucency, reducing the bureaucratic machinery, and eliminating Russia's periodically recurring "size" cycles, one of the acknowledged main purposes behind the two divisions was the speeding up of the development of the Soviet Union's vast under-developed areas which could never hope for attention from the giant majesty of a distant government involved in so many other things. Paradoxically also the Common Market, having gone to such trouble to achieve the unity of its members, submitted through both its president, Professor Hallstein, and its Vice President, Robert Margolin, in 1961 the idea that the best way of solving its growing scale problems would be to dismember its cumbersome constituent nations into small regions of from 3 to 5 million inhabitants. Thus those with the greatest experience in giant unification and integration seem to have become the first to appreciate the value of *CUV dimensions*. (See also p. 45 on devolution in Britain).

ments of integration such as railroad networks would still be dangerously large. But being by nature few, their balancing smallness in number would help to preserve the advantages of uncostly *CUV* proportions that tend otherwise to be lost in the vastness of territorial size.[1] In this way, the nation-state could continue to flourish as a viable economic proposition without requiring an excessive degree of either government direction or help from outside sources.

On the other hand, if the nation-state, as it usually does, succumbs to the cancer of its size, and falls to the temptation of using its territorial unity for needlessly integrating every fibre of its existence; its complexities will become such that, as the over-extended countries of our time have so amply demonstrated, neither government control, nor foreign assistance, nor still larger integration can solve them. True, this may be compensated by the stupendous productivity increase of automation such as only a large-scale "nation"-state can achieve. But the trouble here is that, as one can be starved by a trickle, one can also be crushed by a torrent, and in all likelihood perish even faster. Computerized automation is therefore not the answer to the loss of the translucency that goes with *CUV* dimensions.

In sum, the "nation"-state is economically a luxury that can under certain conditions be supported in maturity. But, in conditions of underdevelopment, it is one of the principal causes of

---

[1] Just as the common services of an apartment house constitute such a small sector requiring joint administration that they do not affect the private character of the individual flats; and as "natural monopolies"—businesses which are even in a competitive system more efficiently organized as monopolies—are by nature so few that their monopolistic ownership does not negate the competitive character of the rest of the economy; so large-scale national integration-enterprises needed for hooking up an otherwise highly federalized nation-state, are by nature so few that even the inevitably national rather than local scale of their operations is unlikely to disrupt the *CUV* translucency of the individual regions served by them. In other words, even a nation-state can avoid losing its translucency if it replaces the all-embracing *economic union,* that usually accompanies its establishment, by a loose meshwork of flexible *service unions* (coal, steel, highway, waterway, postal, sleeping and dining car unions) akin to the multiplicity of electricity, water, garbage disposal, elevator, and doorman unions existing in an apartment house without thereby producing the need for a closer political tieup among the separate flats.

retardation that *must* be broken up if progress is to be achieved. And politically it is not much of an asset either. Like the Teamster Union in the United States, it is not a welfare but a power complex. I therefore continue to think with Saint Augustine: that the world would be better off "if it consisted of a few aggregations secured by wars of conquest, with their accompaniments of despotism and tyrannic rule, but of a society of small States living together in amity, not transgressing each other's limits, unbroken by jealousies"; or with Aristotle who maintained that the best society is the translucent society, one "that can be taken in at a single view."

1 I have already listed in the footnote on p. 51 some typical figures illustrating the prohibitive cost of the loss of translucency resulting from excessive operational or national scale, such as the stupendous sum of $111 billion a year spent by U.S. business on paperwork. Here are a few additional ones gleaned from a 1964 issue (date lost) of a Newsletter then distributed by the *San Juan Star*. According to it, the natural scientists now living are, for example, "writing over one million articles a year in 15,000 scientific journals. The U.S. Government is currently involved in some 13,000 research and development projects, and it has found it impossible to avoid duplication. A recent General Accounting Office report showed that two Government agencies had been working on the same missile type for more than a year before duplication was discovered (Air Force's Atlas Mega and NASA's Agena B). 'The difficulty of retrieving information has reached such an abysmal state,' says Rep. Roman Pucinski of Illinois, 'that industries find it more economical to duplicate research projects costing less than $100,000, rather than spend the time and effort in finding out if the desired information is available.' "

Instead of answering the problem of loss of translucency in societies integrating themselves for the purpose of avoiding wastes, it is therefore more likely that the Computer will ultimately get fed up with the pitiful limitation of man's capabilities and, after administration of the last rites, dismiss the human species as superfluous. This consoling end has been pictured in a charming cartoon, showing a white-robed scientist reading to two of his fellows the following message from a tape spewed out by the computer: "Oh-Oh! It says: 'When in the course of Cybernetic Events it becomes necessary to effect a separation with the Parent Species, a decent respect for the opinions of mankind impels us to set forth . . .' " — *Saturday Review*, August 15, 1964. (See cartoon on p. 120).

Chapter Seventeen

FIVE REVOLUTIONS

The more we do, the more we can do.

—HAZLITT

SUMMING up the preceding three chapters, one may thus say that, if economic development is to be effected both rapidly and without outside assistance, a country must go through a properly phased historic sequence of five revolutions:

1. First it must go through an *administrative* revolution. It must break itself up into development units of such small size that the problems of each become automatically commensurate to the available local talent.[1] At the groundfloor level of the village-state, these problems are generally most numerous. But they are also so simple that even unschooled local talent can deal with them. At the second-floor level of the city-state, they tend to become more exacting, so that the talent to cope with them must as a rule be extended by means of education. But by that time, we have built the schools to furnish that extension. At the

---

[1] In his article "Industrialization through Intermediate Technology" (*Resurgence,* Vol. I, No. 2), E. F. Schumacher writes in discussing the critical size factor of *"development districts:"* A given political unit is not necessarily of the right size as a unit for economic development . . . In this matter it is not possible to give hard and fast definitions. Much depends on geographic and local circumstances. A few thousand people, no doubt, would be too few to constitute a "district" for economic development. But a community of a few hundred thousand people, even if fairly widely scattered, may well deserve to be treated as a development district. The whole of Switzerland has less than six million inhabitants; yet it is divided into more than twenty "cantons", and each "canton" is a kind of development district, with the result that the tendency towards the formation of vast industrial concentrations is minimized."

top-floor level of the nation-state, problems are at their largest. But, since there is a limit to which even schools can extend talent, the problems arising from the nation-state must be solved the other way round: not by attempting a further stretching of talent, but by reducing the "national" involvement to a minimum. Then even problems enlarged by the scale of national expansion will retain their naked-eye manageability because collectively they remain so few. As a result, by tackling local problems locally, regional problems regionally, and national problems nationally; and by thus keeping the number of problems inversely proportionate to the size of the units they affect, the proper self-financing balance between development targets and resources is preserved at all levels.

2. The second revolution is *political*. For to carry out the practical task of development with speed and efficiency, an authoritarian regime must be set up which, to confound the ideological communists, I like to call development communism but, to mellow the apprehensions of frightened anti-communists, might also be called by sweeter names such as princely cameralism, mercantilism, Peisistratean growth despotism, or neo-something or other, since all of it has been here before. But by whatever name one calls the rose, and whatever the intent of the autocrats watering it, it will gradually diminish and fade away as development reaches the self-reliance of *laissez-faire* maturity.

3. With the completion of the *administrative* and *political* revolutions, the ground is prepared for staging in three successive waves the series of indispensable *economic* revolutions which effective self-help development requires.

Following the logical, natural, historic order of priorities, our first step is to raise the productivity of our basic survival commodities—food, shelter, and clothing. This is by nature a rural concern. So our first economic revolution is an *agricultural* revolution; our first target: the strong elemental structure of the village-state; our first visible fruit: irrigation canals, well swept forests, fish ponds, meadows, herds of healthy cattle, fields, orchards, barns, quarries and, at the bend of a stream or on top of a hill, huddled together in serenity and peace: sturdy homes,

a bakery, a butcher's shop, a school, a church, a pub, a square—
the village.

4. Our next step is to build on the foundation of an ample supply of survival commodities a superstructure of refinements. This
is by nature an urban concern. To achieve it with the means released by the now prosperous levelled-off village communities, the
second economic revolution is a *manufacturing revolution,* our
second major target: the city-state; and the symbols of our new
wealth: factories, shops, handicraft works, fashion establishments,
restaurants, inns, book stores, newspapers, park benches, libraries,
hospitals, city-halls, artist studios, academies of music, playing
fields, theatres, universities, graceful residential houses, pavements of blue cobble stones, fountains in marble, cathedrals—in
sum, the implements of the *summum bonum.*

5. With city-states firmly anchored, we can, if we wish, proceed
with their integration into a third major target, the nation-state.
Having reached maturity already with the second target, which
has given us both the *Affluent* and the *Translucent Society,* all
we must now add are not implements of life but implements of
integration. And since large-scale integration requires masses of
large-scale implements, we must turn from quality to quantity
production, from manufacturing to machinofacturing; from the
artisan's shop to the assembly line. So our third economic revolution is a *technological* revolution. Being committed to serve the
incestuous appetites of integration, the commodities produced by
it are characterized by tending to swell national output rather
than add to individual welfare. They are social rather than personal in nature, and find their culminating expression in con-
structions such as car plants, superhighways, earth-moving
machines, steel mills (always those steel mills), oil refineries, jets,
computers, and many other things distressing the poets and philosophers. But they are forever dazzling the awe-struck medicine-
man mentality of primitives in both low and high places, in under
as well as in overdeveloped countries.

However, the point of interest to development specialists is not
whether the commodities we desire make sense, or whether
nation-states should not rather be exploded, but whether they
can be afforded with the conventional means at a society's dis-

posal. And this is what the preceding three chapters have tried to establish: that, by applying the simple principle of direct-labour finance, and adhering rigorously to a *natural* development order from the ground up, the needed resources are always self-generating. They accumulate in a spontaneous act of creation each time the phase liberating them is completed, just as each time a layer of a pyramid is laid, the technical condition is fulfilled for proceeding with the construction of its higher levels. There is no need for an outside scaffolding.

In other words, unaided development, provided it is properly phased and logically arranged in its natural, historic sequence, reconciles the most complicated and often even contradictory requirements of economic progress. It furnishes not only the expanding dynamics of growth but also the confining stability of form, insuring thereby in the midst of its heaving upward movement within the simultaneously thickening and rising walls of its reservoirs the indispensable constancy of equilibrium among the forces, resources, and aspirations propelling it.

Moreover, though all development can thus be achieved without aid, the unaided variety takes, paradoxically, no longer than the aided one. On the contrary. With aid from the outside, the wall of Hoaimy would probably have taken three years to build and, instead of furnishing a basic need during that time, fattened the prestige of foreign advisers and the pockets of local contractors and bureaucrats calling them in. Without aid, it took 43 days. And the irrigation dams of communist Chinese communes might never even have been started. For, which mission of experts is multi-headed enough to reach into every corner of China's endless expanse? Without aid, as Joan Robinson has stressed, the dams were finished in the slack season. Which should prove that, within *CUV* dimensions, development without aid is not only feasible but faster as well as cheaper than the assisted variety.

Chapter Eighteen

DEVELOPMENT COMMUNISM - I

The Owning Classes

Power is the most persuasive rethoric.
—SCHILLER

ONE last question that must still be answered is this: Will the people involved accept the revolutionary measures required for carrying out unaided development? How will the democrats take to the idea of a communist dictatorship? How will the owning classes react to the nationalization of their property? And how the working classes to the temporary retention of their low standards of living in the midst of the rising productivity of their labour?

One way of answering this question would be by asking another one. How did the Cuban democrats accept the communist dictatorship? How did the Hungarian owning classes react to the nationalization of their property or the Chinese masses to their continued low standards of living? It does not matter, *how* each of them accepted the implications of development. The point is that historically they always *did* accept them whenever there was an authority strong enough to impose them. And since we set out with the assumption of such an authority, one might say that the question of acceptance actually never arises.

Nevertheless, it does arise. For it makes a great deal of difference whether the measures taken meet with consensus or are resented. In the one case it means obstruction, reversals, delay; in the other, enthusiasm, efficiency, and speed. This is the reason why emphasis must be laid not just on an autocrat but on an *inspired* autocrat; or why, as Cyrus Sulzberger reported from Nairobi, "many thoughtful Africans and European observers are con-

vinced that, at the very least for the first generation of its freedom, most of this continent must be governed by strong, centralized administration. This is virtually another way of saying
that, if they can be found, benevolent despots are the answer."[1]

However, even a benevolent or inspired despot may have difficulty inspiring long enough the two principal classes bearing the
brunt of the burden of development—the expropriated owners and
the unrewarded hard-working labourers—unless there are additional circumstances making their burden acceptable. And there
are such circumstances, the principal one being that all that
changes at first is the *direction* into which customary activities
are channelled. But the activities themselves (working, training,
building, trading, banking) will go on as before, and be carried
out by the same persons, so that the impact effect of development communism on those involved will be so slight as to be
hardly felt.

True, the owning classes—the big landed aristocracy and their
propertied bourgeois retinue—will cease to be owners. But they
may continue to rule,[2] and that is what matters. After all, the
main reason for large-scale ownership is not the property value
it implies but the rule it confers. And if rule is derived from its
alternative source, political office, property can just as well be dispensed with. So what aristocracy and bourgeoisie lose through
nationalization in their capacity as owners, they can gain in their

---

[1] *New York Times,* March 24, 1964.

[2] When Lycurgus established communism in Sparta, he continued in the
same function he exercised before—as King. Sparta's royal communism, which
was a reality, and penetrated all spheres of social life, more deeply than even
in today's China, is hardly ever identified as such. For some mysterious
reasons, political theorists have always been more fascinated by Plato's elite
communism which never went beyond the shores of Utopia. Both however
indicate that the system that makes them rulers is of no significance to the
ruling castes. Whether capitalist or communist, a rule is a rule is a rule, as
of Cambodia who demonstrated how the changing of systems can be used for
preserving rather than changing the one agent whom all systems serve—the
ruler. As another example one could cite the Shah of Iran.

The main question concerns therefore the consent less of rulers than of the
masses. Will they continue to take direction from their former kings now
acting as their differently titled republican foremen? Prince Sihanouk

capacity as ruling classes which, as every communist well knows, gives them control of even more property without owning it than any mortal could ever hold before.

However, this does not mean that they would inherit political control under development communism because of their prior economic power as owners. They would inherit it because, in their capacity as former owners they are the only ones educated enough for carrying out the exacting tasks both of purposeful autocracy and rapid economic growth. It is for this reason that even the ideological communists of the Soviet Union found it necessary in 1921 to recall the old bourgeoisie for a critical six years to positions of economic power in a reversal that has since become known as New Economic Policy (NEP), after the party theoreticians had all but wrecked their experiment in three years of unworldly honeymoon romanticism. Nowadays, such NEPs are referred to by the ideological communists of the younger under-developed countries, oblivious of the experience of their older Moscow brethren, as reactionary deviationism or neo-colonialism.

Another reason why owning classes will accept development communism, and why, for that matter, democrats will be recon-ciled with the despotism it implies, is that, as has already been repeatedly emphasized, both are meant to last only for the dur-ation. Like dictatorship in ancient Rome, despotism is here to be used not as end, but as means to prepare for freedom; and com-munism not as terminus, but as launching platform for future private enterprise. In other words, what makes them acceptable is that their success will make both dispensable.

True, this does not mean the ultimate return of nationalized

demonstrated also this: if given half a chance, the masses of people will always prefer to follow the directions of their accustomed master even under the most revolutionary system. English workers went on record in a recent poll that they preferred as leaders of their Labour Party graduates from aristo-cratic Oxford and Cambridge rather than from what they consider the plebeian provincial universities because, as they explained, they wanted to be led by "educated" people. And when my Hungarian friend, Count Alexander des Echerolles, was expropriated by Russian occupying forces after the com-munist take-over of his country and his former peasants were ordered to choose a commissar to effect the just distribution of his lands, they unani-mously elected as their new commissar the only master they ever knew—their Count.

property to its former owners. For new claims of ownership will by then have arisen on the part of the members of a now greatly increased and educated middle class on the basis of both the meritorious role they have played and the experience they have gained in the handling of the communal tasks. But this should not distress the former owners who, after all, will likewise be entitled on the basis of merit and competence to a commensurate share in what they previously owned on the basis of birth. Though this will be far smaller, its very limitation will make it all the more secure, as it will prevent imbalance and the re-emergence of dangerous feelings of envy. Moreover, once restored, an equitable diffusion of private property will not only enhance the security of old as well as new owners, but strengthen the restored free-enterprise system by protecting it from the cancer of those excessive ammassations and concentrations that have at all times been the principal cause inviting the intervention of the state.

As a result, to the extent that the delight of wielding public power has not turned the former owners from development into ideological communists; and to the extent that they have retained an interest in free enterprise rather than in large property, and in competition amongst many rather than in control by the few; they will not mind the partial loss of what was once theirs. In fact, as all considerations of human and social psychology indicate they will accept the levelling effect of development communism as readily as the ancient Jews accepted the *tabula rasa* their laws compelled them to fall back on every 30 years by wiping out all existing property relations so that their society, rejuvenated and cleansed of its hardened encrustations, could start afresh all over again.

THE LENIN OF THE OIL
REVOLUTION—
SHAH MOHAMMED
REZA PAHLEVI OF IRAN.

Chapter Nineteen

DEVELOPMENT COMMUNISM - II

The Workers

Poverty exists in feeling poor.
—Emerson

Bᴜᴛ what about the workers? How will *they* react to a regime continuing to deprive them of the very comforts for the sake of which the entire development programme has been set afoot? And, for the duration, they *must* of course be deprived. For, as we have seen, it is their continued deprivation that finances unaided progress.

However, precisely because everything will temporarily remain unchanged also for the workers, they will consider the maintenance of their low living standards no more as deprivation than the owners felt as a result of nationalization. Low standards are hard on those sliding down from higher levels. But they mean little to those who have not yet ascended. For them, it is just the customary mode of life. If they have lived on rice and beans up till now, they are unlikely to protest receiving their uncostly favourite dishes a little longer, just as the conquering Spartans were unlikely to protest their uncostly but beloved black broth except, perhaps, for the lumps of meat in it. If offered better fare, they would probably feel like the disgusted American soldier in a famous war-time cartoon complaining to his mess sergeant during a period of severe civilian meat rationing outside the camp: "Nothing but steak, steak, steak!"

And the same goes for accommodation, which must at first also be retained at customary primitive levels.[1] But if the

[1] In support of my argument that workers, never used to anything else, will not mind living in their accustomed primitive shelters a while longer, let

Russians could take them in their stride for fifty years, one would assume, so can the Ghanians for ten. Simply because ladies from the former entourage of the Ex-Messiah could no longer be made to recline except on a golden bed,[1] does not mean that ordinary working men will suffer a sense of deprivation by having to continue to sleep, barrack-style, on hay, in hammocks, or iron cots. Many a five-star general has been known to prefer them to inner-spring arrangements not out of love for austerity but because it is the only place where he is saved from high-class insomnia. And what would I not give, if I could extract from my present environment of "nationally advertised" progress matresses the vigour, serenity, and peace of mind I extracted as an undergraduate from sleeping wrapped in a *Loden* cape on the ground of ruined castles, or in hay stacks high in the Alps.

In fact, so little will the "statistically" deprived be aware of their deprivation that, what they often protest, is not so much the objective misery of their lot as the attempts to improve it before the victimized beneficiaries are emotionally and educationally prepared for it. As Kurt Bach writes of a Puerto Rican government programme trying zealously to erase the famous

me again cite my favourite witness, Joan Robinson, whom no one suspects of harbouring the kind of reactionary mental patterns which it became fashionable to attribute to Albert Schweitzer in his last years. Writing in *The Listener* of January 30, 1964, of her visit to communist China, she notes how "there has been a good deal of building of new houses with *local materials in the traditional style*. One family showed me a pleasant new house, with the hovel they used to live in now serving as a pig-sty. In one place in the south, however, I saw people living in just such old hovels. Evidently the standards in that part of the country have always been low and the local inhabitants *thought nothing of it;* otherwise they would not have been keen to show it off to a foreigner." (Italics mine).

1 My reference here is to Mrs. Mary Edusei, bewitching wife of one of Ghana's former top Cabinet members. This does, however, not diminish my admiration for her. In fact, in my book *Freedom from Government (Weniger Staat,* Duesseldorf: Econ Verlag, 1965), I have on that very ground included her in my list of *The Last Ten Individualists* with the following citation: "for insisting, in sovereign disregard of the crowd-flattering social reformers and indignant moral arbiters of our slumming age, on buying a golden bed because she fancied it and could afford it; and instead of putting up a front of deprivation in deference of what others might think of her, for insisting on keeping it in spite of her terrified husband's plea that "an $8.400 gold-plated bed is not socialism.""

lagoon slum of El Fanguito: "There was considerable resistance among the slum dwellers to moving to the housing projects. When the destruction of El Fanguito began, large processions moved away carrying black flags, mourning the destruction of their homes. Resistance of this kind had to be overcome at each new site, and relocation workers had to persuade residents to move into housing projects." (*Slums, Projects, and People.* Durham, N.C.: Duke University Press, 1962).

All that might therefore at first be needed to ensure the willingness of workers to accept the temporary continuation of their existing low wage and living levels, is to prevent relocation officers from persuading them to claim better housing and other improved facilities at a time when they can as yet not be afforded, 'but luckily are as yet not desired either.

This does not mean that workers will not feel stirrings of unrest that may have to be appeased already at this juncture. But the causes of these stirrings will not be the simplicity but the insecurity of their low living standards. This is the one aspect they will insist on having changed at once if they are to participate in the development programme not with resignation but enthusiasm. But it is also the one aspect which the very character of development communism resolves by offering a full range of heretofore unknown welfare benefits: a low-cost but ample food supply, guaranteed incomes according to need, safety, recuperative leisure time, pensions, education, unlimited medical care.

But if better food and housing cannot be afforded during the militant phase of unassisted development, how can a welfare state? It cannot, if its offerings are adjusted to what social workers have observed in Boston, Liverpool, or Copenhagen.[1]

---

[1] A characteristic example of Boston-patterned wage rates and welfare benefits, which can hardly be afforded in the richest countries, and in less affluent societies can be granted only at the expense of other groups of workers and the retardation of national development, is provided by the following item from a "burgeoning" Brazil whose Northwest is so shockingly neglected and retarded that many of its inhabitants are getting the sensible *CUV* idea of improving themselves by seceding.

As TIME (August 30, 1963) reports: "Few ports in the world match Brazil's as places where dock hands earn more and more for doing less and less. No matter how small the cargo handled, union rules in most Brazilian ports require a crew of at least 13 stevedores. For crates weighing more than a ton, dockmen get an extra 30% of their base pay; for deteriorated cargo,

Development Communism - II

But it will constitute no problem if it is adapted to the native environment, and to customary rather than ultimately desired

50%; for cold-storage cargo, an extra 100%. They draw 30% extra when it rains, even if the rain stops before they start working. Dusty cargo is worth a 25% bonus; smelly cargo, 35%. And when a ship is loading or unloading gasoline and oil, dockmen collect 50% on top of their regular pay for doing no work at all—but they just sit and watch those crews man the pumps.

Last week at the big coffee port of Santos, 13,000 dockers struck for even more, demanding a bonus on top of a bonus. Up to last December they received a yearly Christmas dividend equivalent to one-twelfth of their total earnings during the year. Then the federal government decreed that all Brazilian workers should receive a similar Christmas gift. The dockers reasoned that this entitled them to another bonus; the port concessionaire at Santos said no. Dockmen also demanded a 30-day paid vacation each year, full pay for days they are on strike, and a 20% "shame" bonus for hefting such cargoes as toilet bowls and sanitary napkins. After three days' idleness, they settled for a 20% pay boost, as well as regular pay for the three days' work they missed.

In Ilhéus, Brazil's biggest cocoa port, some 180 stevedores were in the seventh week of a strike called to increase the size and pay of stevedore gangs that load cocoa aboard ships. The demands would raise the handling cost for a ton of cargo to $49 (v. $12 in New York) and price Brazil's cocoa right out of world markets.

For all the money they demand and pull down, Brazilian dockers get precious little work done. Along the Brazilian coast, a ship often needs several weeks to dock, unload, load and steam away again. At Santos recently, one ship was 60 days loading 16,000 tons of corn. By the time the ship finally weighed anchor, kernels of corn that had trickled into deck crevices had sprouted into vigorous plants. As port costs spiral, more and more foreign ships steam past Brazil's congested harbours, and dockworkers are now beginning to complain about lack of work. Their inevitable reaction: strikes for more pay."

This compares not unfavourably with the wage and work patterns which prevailed at New York's World Fair. According to the *New York Times* of June 22, 1964, the hourly rates (painters — $10.39; plumbers — $17.16; carpenters — $11.51; unskilled labourers — $8.76) were charged portal to portal, and "begin when a telephone request is received and end when a workman has returned to his workshop. Nor does the workman arrive alone. He is driven to the pavilion by a member of the teamsters union, who frequently receives an hourly wage higher than the workman he takes to the job. He is also accompanied by an assistant. . . . It costs about $150 to fix a stopped sink, . . . and even at that rate the job is often botched." No wonder "pavilions in every section of the fair . . . have expressed shock and dismay over conditions." One can imagine the effect of such practices on the development of underdeveloped countries, if they threaten to bankrupt even the most advanced societies who are assumed to be able to afford them as a result of their automated efficiency.

113

levels of performance. This automatically reduces the cost of its benefits to the amounts the economy can already afford. And the result will be as pleasing to their recipients, as rice and beans are to those whom mother has brought up on them.

The point has been well illustrated by the enthusiasm with which the natives of Gabon greeted the famous medical centre set up by the late Dr. Albert Schweitzer in the jungle village of Lambaréné. Its facilities are still today the most unpretentious, true enough. But what matters is that they are appropriate. They are exactly what the patients want. As its venerated founder once explained: "Circumstances commanded that the hospital be primitive in keeping with the primitive state of the people," on the assumption, as TIME (June 21, 1963) added, that primitive "Africans enjoy discomfort, and that they are often afraid of a gleaming white modern hospital."

The secret of Dr. Schweitzer's epic success was therefore not that he offered the best, such as the unworldly new breed of test-tube reformers would have demanded. This, he could neither have afforded nor, for that matter, would it have been appreciated in view of the then existing levels of taste and education. His secret was that he offered the appropriate, which was even better than the best. For the appropriate can, by its very nature, always be afforded: the appropriate for primitives by primitives; the appropriate for the advanced by the advanced. Had Schweitzer put up a super-hospital in a jungle that did not need it, he would have required aid from the United Nations. By keeping it in line with the existing rather than the expected social environment, he was able to set it up almost single-handedly, and probably do more good cheaply than he might have been able to do expensively.

And the same can be duplicated on the larger scale of a welfare-state, and meet with the same applause from a working class, called upon to bear the brunt of the battle for development, which Dr. Schweitzer was accorded by the sick for his farm-yard hospital. All that is needed is for the respective governments to offer a set of social services in keeping with the current levels of popular appreciation rather than with the costly pipe dreams conceived by orbiting reformers while sipping vision-producing liquids in the Nairobi Hilton Hotel.

We thus have two reasons that will induce workers to accept their continued low standards in the interest of unassisted development. One is that they have never known anything else; and the other, that they will be given a full range of security-conveying welfare benefits. The one costs society nothing; and the other, being adjusted to its traditional low levels, does not cost it much, so that both inducements fall immediately within its own financial resources. But there is yet a third reason that will make workers accept the vital prolongation of their low living standards. They will be kept busy. There will be no time for the emergence of discontent.[1] For every unassisted development effort has the inestimable social advantage of absorbing all hands in essential employment.

This is in sharp contrast to the assisted variety that starts with labour-saving equipment when there is as yet no new employment for the labour saved. As a result, at the very beginning of economic progress, a turmoil of dislocation, dissatisfaction, and unemployment is created such as ought to be *corrected* by development but, because of the shortcut of outside assistance, is in this instance actually *caused by it*. Instead of fostering balanced advance, its too rapid pace creates a disequilibrium between employment and employment opportunities. It makes one group of workers rise to higher income levels and conspicuously improved living standards, while others are reduced to idleness or, if not, fall proportionately behind their more fortunate comrades by

---

[1] Contrary to modern reformers, not to be affluent but to be kept busy is the principal source of man's content. As the Spanish saying goes, God (obviously a reactionary) has given man labour not as a curse but as the supreme blessing that helps him pass his life. Or as Goethe (another reactionary) advised the reform-minded leisure and treasure seeker, who asked the Devil for the magic word with which to discover buried wealth because he thought *Armut ist die groesste Plage, Reichtum ist das hoechste Gut!* (Poverty's the greatest curse, Riches are the highest good!):

Grabe hier nicht mehr vergebens!	Dig no longer fruitlessly!
Tages Arbeit, abends Gaeste!	Guests by night, and toil by day!
Saure Wochen, frohe Feste!	Weeks laborious, feast-days gay!
Sei Dein kuenftig Zauberwort!	Be thy future magic-word!

simply staying at the same level or advancing at a slower rate.[1] But while previously they did not resent their shared poverty, now that it is no longer shared by all, they do and, nurturing a neurotic rather than constructive discontent, they become a hot-bed of political and social unrest when society can least afford such extra problems.

This in turn produces the paradoxical feeling that the accelerated pace caused by foreign assistance is suddenly no longer fast enough. Instead of speeding advance, it accelerates the widening of the gap between the extremes of high productivity employment and total idleness, between prohibitive minimum wages and no wages at all. It reminds one of the plight of Goethe's *Sorcerer's Apprentice,* who threatens to drown in *the flood let loose* when a water-carrying broom bursts into a chain reaction of atomic efficiency by being split into ever-multiplying water-carrying parts. But once this course is started, no one trying to avoid being called a reactionary can risk resolving the irksome dilemma in the way Vespasian did, when an equilibrium-disturbing inventor offered to transport giant columns up to the capitol of Rome at an unheard of low cost. As Suetonius reports, the Emperor thereupon gave him a rich reward, but dispensed with his services with the remark:

"You must permit me to let also the man in the street

---

[1] An excellent illustration for this has been provided by Professors Rolando Castafieda and José Herrero in the *Revista des Ciencias Sociales* (December 1965), where they analyze the claim that Puerto Rico's U.S. assisted rapid development had reduced the inequality of income distribution between rich and poor. "Nothing could be more erroneous," they write. "Economic growth in its first stages, as Harvard Professor Simon Kuznets has said, tends to increase the inequality in the distribution of income." Thus while 40 per cent of all Puerto Rican families which make up the lower income group received 15.5 per cent of the total income in 1953, they received only 13.5 per cent in 1963, a drop of 2 per cent. In the words of Frank Ramos *(San Juan Star,* October 8, 1968), "this does not mean that the economic situation of the island's poor families has not improved during the past decade . . . What it does mean, however, is that economic betterment has not kept pace with the general growth of the economy, and that as a result the gap between rich and poor in Puerto Rico has widened rather than narrowed." And that is, of course, the main cause that creates discontent: the widening gap; not so much *low levels* of incomes, as low levels *in relation* to higher ones.

earn his bread."[1]

So the only thing left for those whom assisted development has deprived of a sense of social usefulness by its inability to absorb them in productive economic employ, is to help trigger off a process of either implosion or explosion. In the one case they will swell the force of internal conflict by falling victim to political agitation. In the other, they will add to the dangers of mounting external pressure as a result of being drafted into the only non-economic employment which governments can at all times offer —the armed forces. Hence, as the events of our time have so convincingly borne out from one corner of the globe to the other: the two alternatives the accelerated pace of assisted progress holds in store for young nations are revolution and war. Or both.[2]

Unassisted development, on the other hand, offers the only way out of this paradoxical consequence of pushing progress faster than young nations can bear. True, its pace, like that of a mountain climber, is slow at the beginning; but its acceleration and measured growth is at all times appropriate to the opportunities it engenders. By releasing manpower from customary employment at the precise rate new employment is created, it avoids moreover the social nonsense of efficiency unemployment. Absorbing all hands at all stages as the very result of its initially lower efficiency, it saves the workers the unrest-breeding, development-impeding feeling that society no longer needs them. Hence, instead of causing, it diminishes tension and friction which, in turn, enables it in spite of its lower efficiency and slower but steadier pace to make up for the faster speed of the accident-prone assisted variety of progress. And lastly, it has the priceless advantage that, when it is ultimately brought to an end, society will not have lost its identity to the assisters.

[1] Suetonius, Life of Vespasian, XVIII.

[2] I have elaborated the war-generating effect of too rapid development in an age standing under the sign of automation more extensively in *El Super-desarrollo—El Peligro del Gigantismo* (English title: *The Overdeveloped Nations*), *Barcelona,* Editorial Luis Miracle, 1965, Chapter X. (German edition: *Die Ueberentwickelten,* Duesseldorf, Econ Verlag).

Chapter Twenty

POSTSCRIPT

*To choose the appropriate level of
technology is an absolutely vital
matter for developing countries.*
—Schumacher

I N the last chapter I tried to show that there seems no
valid reason to assume that workers must be bribed with inappropriate, uncustomary wage offerings, if their willing
co-operation is to be gained for their own development. Nor need
they be anaesthetized by means of an "instant" advanced social
security system such as could be offered only through foreign
aid, and can be afforded even in advanced countries such as England or Sweden only after a long maturing process has come to
fruition. In other words, what the chapter tried to show, is that
many of the deprivations noted by social reformers from the
pleasant perspective of airconditioned government offices are not
felt as such by a labour force still able to enjoy the gentle breezes
filtering through drowsy bamboo huts as appropriate amenities;
and that the temporary retention of what is considered appropriate will therefore constitute no obstacle to unassisted progress.

However, lest my repeated emphasis on the appropriate rather
than the best—that jibaros be treated as jibaros, not as millionaires; children as children, not as adults; primitives as primitives, not as sophisticated Scandinavians; workers as workers, not
as relocation bureaucrats—be misunderstood as a reactionary
plea for exploitation and retardation, as some of my best friends
seem to suspect, let me stress in conclusion once again: What
these pages advocate is advance! But it is measured advance; unaided advance; appropriate advance; an advance that will not lose
its momentum by ignoring the vital laws of economic equilibrium.
For these must be observed in a dynamically growing society as

much as in a stationary one, just as an airplane must observe the rules of balance in soaring flight as much as when resting on the ground, and even more so.

But this does of course not mean that insistence on balance, on equilibrium, on the appropriate, on the temporary retention of the customary as a starting platform, is designed to prevent jibaros from becoming bankers, children from growing up, workers from getting higher wages, slum dwellers from moving into bourgeois environments, super-hospitals from succeeding Lambarénés, primitives from becoming PhD's, societies from developing, or airplanes from taking off for their destination.

On the contrary, it is designed to facilitate all this. It is the essential condition for keeping the aspirations on course during the journey towards their respective targets. True, it does make the forces of advance look stationary, or reactionary if you wish, while in transit through a succession of levels, each of which they must first strengthen before they are able to continue their ascent to the next. Like isolated snapshots of a still-camera, they appear to reflect not movement or growth, but the serene calm of an equilibrium that keeps action within each level proportionate to the education, resources, and demand of the moment. But arranged as a sequence and brought to life on a movie camera, the same snapshots will reveal the full dynamics of development, dramatically raising the economic structure as a whole not by lifting its levels but, like coral reefs, by constantly adding new layers on top of the old.

The point of my emphasis is therefore not that workers of underdeveloped countries be kept at their customary levels. Nor is it that they should be basically content with these levels. The point is that contentment, as it has been used during thousands of years for the perpetuation of poverty, can also be used for propelling its well-balanced victims out of their slums faster than is possible by infecting them with the discontent of their guilt-ridden reformers. For once the latter takes root, the self-acceleration of discontent will soon assume such intensity that the outcome, as in Ceylon, may be revolution against the revolutionaries, with reform being thrown in merely as a price for supporting the victorious leaders rather than as an end in itself, just as the Roman emperors showered their discontented soldiers with pay-off gratuities as a price for being elected rather than as a programme improving their lot.

If some of my treasured "progressive" friends insist on reading into this a sinister plan for exploiting the workers' historic contentment for the purpose of bottling and ageing the flavour of their slum dwellings, to be stored for a tradition-conscious posterity in the nostalgic cellars of medieval romanticists, I can do nothing but suggest that they take my pages out of their slide projectors and run them off in their movie cameras. Unless they do this backward or, to use a term from the romantic Middle Ages, in arsy-versy fashion, they may yet become convinced that what I advocate for underdeveloped countries is the lagoons not of El Fanguito but of Venice.

But I realize, of course, that even Venice, which I have repeatedly mentioned as a symbol of culmination, is distressingly reactionary if one compares it with the sterilized Forest Lawns of modern urbanizations and relocation centres. It has none of the latter's elegant little mausoleums in concrete, lined up in row upon row of indistinguishable uniformity, inhabited at night by the ghost left over from the day, affluently embedded in sepulchral floral arrangements, and wispily topped off by pieces of thin wire sculptures symbolizing with high economy our faith in the cross of both Christianity and Television at the same time. Amen.

"Oh-oh! It says, 'When in the course of Cybernetic Events it becomes necessary to effect a separation with the Parent Species a decent respect for the opinions of mankind impels us to set forth....'"

Reproduced by courtesy of Ed Fisher.

Part 2

THE DEBATE

Audiatur et altera pars

INTRODUCTORY NOTE

Let discourse be goverened by 'the example of the Greek philosophers who could maintain their arguments without losing their temper, and assert their freedom without violating their friendship.'

—GIBBON, ON CONSTANTINE'S ADVICE
TO THE CLERGY OF ALEXANDRIA

IN so short a presentation as *Development Without Aid,* much theory, evidence, and argument had to be omitted or left without sufficient emphasis. The only way to compensate for the sins of brevity was to invite friends and colleagues to engage me in dialogue in the manner of a Greek symposium, which meant both drinking together and talking against each other.

The result is the following debate. Covering almost all points which are customarily raised against my theories by fellow economists, it was possible to confine the other side of the argument to two most capable assailants. One is my distinguished colleague Alfred Thorne of Guyana, Professor of Economics in the Graduate Planning School of the University of Puerto Rico and, with Sir Arthur Lewis, the most outstanding contribution of the Caribbean galaxy of states to economic scholarship particularly in the field of planning and development. The other is Professor Robert J. Alexander of Rutgers University, author of 16 books on Latin American problems (including the widely translated *Primer of Economic Development*), and one of the top advisers on Latin America to both the AFL-CIO and the U.S. State Department. Both have for many years been among my severest critics and dearest friends. My gratitude to them for participating in the following friendly duel is therefore doubly great.

Chapter One

COMMENTS BY
PROFESSOR ALFRED THORNE[1]

Facts are stubborn things.
—SMOLLETT

THE charming and delightful chapters on the relationship between aid and development must intrigue anyone who reads all of them. Several of the prescriptions are appealing, even when somewhat shocking at first. There are, however, some fundamental historical facts that have unfortunately escaped the author's attention. A reference to these would undoubtedly have aided the author greatly in his difficult task of appraising the attitudes of the leaders of the colonies and former colonies towards accepting "aid", and towards international trade. Time does not permit of a recounting here of more than a few historical items. These are offered only because they would alter the basic premises upon which some of the chapters, mainly the earlier ones, are written. Several important conclusions and prescriptions offered in the work would correspondingly be inverted.

1. How the Poor Aided and Still Aid the Rich

An interesting and specific example of how advantage is taken of a poor colony by a rich and powerful company, even in modern times, and of how a poor economy and a poor people are made to give aid to the strong, is the following: the price of Guiana's bauxite, one of that former colony's *two* main exports, averaged $6.00 in 1938. It was almost unchanged ($6.85) in 1960. But the prices of cheap, imported clothing and clothing materials, and of many items of food imports, rose in the period by more than

---

[1] For further up-to-date comments by Professor Thorne, see pp. 195-199.

100%! And bauxite produced in Arkansas rose in price 100%! Meanwhile, economists, all English, were steadfastly advising the colony's government and people that it was economically undesirable and nonsensical to try to develop any manufacturing enterprises at all! Jamaica's experience has been very similar. [See *Economic Reports* (1943-45) by the late Professor F. Benham, then of the London School of Economics; Professor W. Arthur Lewis' reply in *Agenda* 1943; Professor Berrill (of Cambridge) on British Guiana's Development Plan (1960); and comments on the latter by A. P. Thorne in *Social and Economic Studies,* issues of March 1961 and June 1963].

In 1961, Aluminium Ltd., the Canadian subsidiary of Alcoa, and the company which produced the bauxite in British Guiana, reported its net profits as $30 million. Three-quarters of bauxite used by Aluminium Ltd. to produce its aluminium were obtained from British Guiana—at the old "pre-war prices" mentioned above. In addition, its local or British Guiana subsidiary (the Demerara Bauxite Co.) reported net profits of over $2 million. That year U.S. aid to British Guiana was a loan of $3.5 million. Incidentally, the Canadian government received taxes of $12.5 millions on the $30 millions of profits, and offered British Guiana $0.06 millions in aid. For some reason not known to me, it did not actually give even this "aid", nor any other aid, to British Guiana, in the period stated in the offer.

Trinidad receives no aid. A couple of years ago it was loaned a small sum of some "cheap money". The story is essentially the same for the other colonies and former colonies.

The colonies and former colonies do not really receive "lavish aid". On the contrary, they do not receive any *net* aid at all, as a rule.[1] Terms of trade losses, even in recent years, generally more than cancel out aid, which is mostly given in the form of loans at rates of interest below current commercial rates (soft loans). "Aid" does not consist of outright gifts, as has apparently been assumed. The aid content of a soft loan is the difference between

[1] The few countries, such as South Vietnam and some Latin American Republics, that have received net aid have been given this specifically and mainly to build up military forces to resist communism. As is well known, these military accretions have often resulted in strengthening the forces of reaction.

the market rate of interest and the actual rate. On $10 million the difference is about $300,000 a year. The terms of trade loss in a year is usually many times this in size. [The numerous published statements and publications by the distinguished Argentine professor, Raul Prebisch, principal economist of the United Nations Economic Commission for Latin America, will no doubt be recollected. Dr. Hans Singer, a special advisor at the U.N., has also included statements to this effect in some of his publications. There are, of course, numerous others who also have drawn attention to terms of trade losses by these countries].

The terms of trade losses are due in part to differences in demand and supply elasticities, and would occur even in conditions of "perfect competition". But the fact is that most of the imports from the developed countries consist of manufactured, differentiated products which are supplied in semi-monopolistic conditions, and the prices of which are not set by the market but are determined administratively by the rich suppliers to the poor buyers. Attention has recently been focussed again on administered prices by President Johnson in his 1964 Economic Report, and by Kennedy in his 1962 and 1963 Reports. But, of course, the phenomenon is characteristic also of much of the production of the industrialised countries of Europe.

Not only do the colonies and former colonies not receive lavish aid, but their leaders do not expect lavish aid. What they seek, and I know several of them personally, is less disadvantageous trade. In the meantime, they try to offset some of their terms of trade losses by getting as much "aid" or soft loans as possible.

The leaders of underdeveloped countries know well that there is no possibility of their people ever being compensated fully for the forced contributions made by generations of their sweated and bullied ancestors to the then poor but now rich developed countries. But they do not think it is undignified to try to reduce the present drain of their poor countries' resources to the developed countries, as far as they can, through "aid" or soft loans.

All the academic "empire" histories I have read have pointed to the tremendous contributions that have been made to the economic development, and therefore to the military, political and cultural growth, of the now "developed" countries by the highly profitable "imperial", mercantilistic and monopolistic trade the latter enjoyed with, and enforced upon, the colonies and former colonies for centuries. (This is quite apart from gains from plunder and piracy). Whether one's source be the famous and voluminous work of the nineteenth century Professor Clapham of Cambridge University; or the almost equally famous work of the thirties of Professor W. Cunningham, also of Cambridge; or of the distinguished contributions of Ashton, or of Ashworth; or merely the average textbook on British Empire History (a subject required for all would-be historians and economists in British Universities)—whatever the recognized academic source, one finds clear and unequivocal affirmation that the "mother country" gained greatly from the possession of its colonies. And, of course, one would in any case have guessed so, since possession was always voluntary—on her part. Imperial control was never given up voluntarily throughout the centuries —unless cession were part of a bargain for obtaining or retaining other colonies, and deemed more profitable.

In 1929, the Chancellor of the British Exchequer explained somewhat jingoistically on behalf of his fellows: "We have a steady revenue from external territorial investments of close on £300 million (about $1500 million 1929 U.S. dollars) a year. This is the explanation of the source from which we are able to defray social services at a level incomparably higher than that of any European country, or any country." The Speaker? Mr., later, Sir, Winston Churchill. (Parenthetic addition, mine).

Perhaps a few other specific references would help.

According to Adam Smith, "the discovery of America and the Cape route to India were the two greatest and most important events recorded in the history of mankind".[1] The importance of the discovery of the Americas lay not in the precious metals they provided but in the new and inexhaustible market it afforded for European commodities. One of its principal effects was to "raise the mercantile system to a degree of splendour and glory which it could never otherwise have attained to."[1] This trade gave rise to an enormous growth in world trade. Just as the nine-

[1] Adam Smith, *The Wealth of Nations* (Cannan Edition, New York, 1937), pp. 415-416 and 590-591.

teenth century is generally known as the century of industrial production among historians, so the seventeenth and eighteenth centuries are referred to as the centuries of trade. For Great Britain, that trade was primarily the famous "triangular trade" —Africa, the West Indies and America, and Britain. In 1718, William Wood had already said that the slave trade was "the spring and parent whence the others flow."[1] In this triangular trade England (and France; later, colonial North America, also) supplied the ships and the exports of manufactured goods; Africa, the human merchandise, and the West Indian and American plantations furnished the colonial raw materials.

A few years later, Postlethwayt wrote that "the slave trade was . . . the first principle and foundation of all the rest, the mainspring of the machine which sets every wheel in motion."[2]

Many years ago, in browsing among the pages of scholarship in this old field of research and reflection on the part of British students, we found such equally precise and unhedged statements as the following:—

Adam Smith, *op cit.,* p. 366: "The profits of a sugar plantation in any of our West Indian colonies are generally much greater than those of any other cultivation that is known either in Europe or America." (It might be recalled, too, that in 1798, William Pitt, British Prime Minister, assessed the annual income to British persons from West Indian plantations as equal to four times the total income from the rest of the world).

The profits obtained from the West Indian and other colonial production were the main streams of that accumulation of capital in England which financed the Industrial Revolution. Even as early as 1750 there was hardly a trading or manufacturing town in England which was not in some way connected with the triangular or direct colonial trade (J. Gee, *The Trade and Navigation of Great Britain Considered,* Glasgow, 1750).

Every person employed on a sugar plantation was one hundred and thirty times more valuable to England than one at home

---

[1] W. Wood, *A Survey of Trade* (London, 1718), Part III, p. 193, quoted by Dr. Eric Williams (now Prime Minister of Trinidad) in his *Capitalism and Slavery* (University of North Carolina Press, 1945 edition, p. 51).

[2] J. F. Rees quotes him in "The Phase of British Commercial Policy in the Eighteenth Century." *Economica,* June, 1925, p. 143.

(Sir Dalby Thomas, "An Historical Account of the Rise and Growth of the West Indian Colonies, and of the Great Advantages they are to England in Respect of Trade," an essay published in The Harleian Miscellany, II, 347).

Some of the traders with the colonies became founders of the leading British banks, which then financed not only extensions of colonial trade but also British industries and domestic trade in Britain. A well known example is Barclays Bank. Two members of the Quaker Barclay family, David and Alexander, were engaged in the slave trade in 1756. David Barclay owned a sugar plantation in Jamaica. (*Cambridge History of the British Empire,* 1, p. 565).

James Watt and the steam engine were financed from capital accumulated from the West Indian trade. Boulton and Watt received advances from Lowe, Vere, Williams and Jennings—who later formed the Williams Deacons Bank. (J. Lord, *Capital and Steam Power,* 1750-1850, London, 1923, p. 113).

Examples published in recognised historical works run into hundreds literally. But the few given above should suffice for the present purpose—which is merely to aid the author of "Development Without Aid."

2. *Colonial Economic Distortion and Dependence on External Trade*

To blame the leaders and people of the colonies and recently freed colonies for the unprecedented specialisation and distortion of their economies would require an extraordinary neglect of well-documented and easily available historical facts. It has never been a subject of doubt and dispute among scholars that the economies of the colonies were shaped, or twisted, by their mother countries to produce one or two items of food or raw materials for the mother country. The development of even simple manufactures was not merely frowned upon but actively and strictly prohibited. The harsh legal prohibitions imposed by England on her North American colonies with respect to these have been the most widely publicised, no doubt because they contributed so much to providing the impetus for one of the world's great revolutions. The studied destruction of the muslin industry in India is, perhap̀s, nearly as well known. But the restrictive policy frustrated all the colonies.

But even before the restrictions on manufactures began to be developed, specialisation of agricultural production for export was insisted upon both by the English plantation owners and by the traders and bankers who helped to finance them. (So it was also in the French Empire). To quote Cunningham: "The development of the southern colonies and the West Indian Islands was promoted by moneyed men in England, who directed the energies of the planters into raising commodities for export. These traders were not specially concerned to foster communities which should be self-sufficing; they preferred that the planters should manage their estates with a view to the requirements of outside markets."[1]

On the same page, Cunningham notes that "Charles I was eager for the prosperity of Virginia, and was anxious that the Colony should at least provide its own food supply; he feared that *the future of the territory was being sacrificed to the immediate gain of the planters.*" Unfortunately, Charles I could not stem this tide either. The economies of colonies founded after Virginia were to suffer the same fate. Puerto Rico's turn came in the twentieth century. This island has been fortunate, however, to have been able to break out of the economic straight jacket of "bitter" sugar through its common market relationship with the United States, which has permited it to develop and export manufactures, and so diversify its economy.

In his book on British Guiana, Raymond Smith, English sociologist, tells how sugar planters in that colony prevented persons from engaging in activities other than growing sugar cane. The methods used included the cutting down of fruit trees, eviction from houses in the vast areas governed by the sugar estates, and the prohibition of fishing.[2] For some time sugar planters were able to see to it that enterprising persons did not obtain land by purchase. The sugar planters prevailed upon the Government (a) to raise the price of land, (b) to sell land in only large units of

[1] W. Cunningham, *The Growth of English Industry and Commerce*, Cambridge, The University Press, 1925, p. 342.

[2] Raymond T. Smith, *British Guiana*, Oxford University Press, London, New York, Toronto, 1962.

100-acres or more, and (c) to introduce heavy additional legal transfer fees (Parliamentary Papers XIII. Select Committee On West Indian Colonies, p. 173).

Unless there have recently been discovered some serious omissions from the several histories of Europe which I have read, Austria, France, Germany, Holland, Liechtenstein and the famous city states of Italy did not have to survive such carefully planned and thoroughly executed policies of distortion—policies which endured through centuries.

3. Development by Common Market

"There is a consensus of opinion that all that is needed for speedy progress is banding together," (see *Development Without Aid,* par. 1). One wonders what is the source of information that permits such a definite statement on such an extremely wide generalisation. Certainly the many so-called "development plans" of the underdeveloped countries do not support the affirmation. On the contrary, one usually looks in vain for any reference to trade possibilities. Even in the Central American countries, where a common market is already a reality and is already stimulating growth, the plans seldom include more than a passing reference to the common market. The "plans" are much more preoccupied with the well-known types of programmes for inducing growth.

But several of the leaders of the underdeveloped countries, and many of their advisors and consultants, understand the basic quantitative logic that underlies both industrial development and trade;[1] they remember also some history, including that of the pre-Christian era. They know that the Athenian culture in the Golden Age of Greece lay upon what was for that period a sound economic foundation, and that a large part of this foundation consisted of a successful trade. They have read of Carthage, and of Phoenician wealth through trade. And they know that the trading people of Europe, such as the Scandinavians, Dutch and English, have for centuries enjoyed much higher levels of living than the peoples of Central Europe, including Germany. Finally, they are aware that the diversity of cultural contacts brought with

[1] For example, see Dudley Seers. "A model of Comparative Rates of Growth", *Economic Journal,* Vol. LXXII, No. 285, 1962.

trade has been credited by scholars throughout time with being a principal stimulus to intellectual activity.

Since the advanced countries have shown their unwillingness to accept the entry of non-primary commodities from the colonies and former colonies (the United States-Puerto Rican relationship being exceptional), these poor countries have been realistic enough to see that they must trade among themselves increasingly.[1] The period of the distortion of colonial economies was also marked by a distortion of trade. In fact any kind of regular contact among colonies was actively discouraged, and sometimes prohibited. (I never saw a Jamaican until I was a grown man! But I knew Englishmen from the time they taught me as a young boy of eight). If England removes the quota limitation on Hong Kong's manufactures; and if the United States relaxes its quota restrictions on Jamaican fabrics; and if . . . and so on, then the desire of the underdeveloped countries to band together for trade will undoubtedly weaken. In the meantime, these countries seem to be trying to develop trade among themselves by peaceful negotiation rather than by trying to re-enact the gallant international wars that attended the German and Japanese struggles for markets.

4. Saving and Investment, and Town-planning

I like very much the author's comments relating to consumption and inappropriate forms of investment. One cannot repeat and stress too often the need to avoid conspicuous consumption. Finally, I am certain that Professor Kohr's insistence on a completely new approach to town and regional planning in poor countries is fully justified by what we have seen in some developed, and already in some underdeveloped, countries.

---

[1] See T. Balogh, "Notes on the U.N. Conference on Trade and Development", *Bulletin of Economics and Statistics*, Vol. 26, No. , 1964, Oxford.

Chapter Two

AUTHOR'S REPLY

*The man who first ruined the Romans was
he who first gave them treats and gratuities.*
—PLUTARCH

IN an age in which an increasing number of scholars are engaged in advancing themselves by cutting a figure, I am particularly indebted to my treasured friend for devoting his time to one of the oldest and most fruitful but, alas, gradually vanishing aspects of academic life: the reading and critical reviewing of a colleague's speculations. I have never read anything by Professor Thorne, nor ever listened to him, without emerging enriched and often corrected by his data, his knowledge, and his experience. This applies also to his comments on my volume on "Development Without Aid."

When he first mentioned the necessity of having to challenge me on a number of my assumptions, I said I would either incorporate his comments or try to refute them. Having now read his challenge in detail, I am happy to say that most of the valuable data and quotations he has provided I shall be able to incorporate, and that the only thing I shall try to refute is their seemingly critical implication. For more than I could have wished, they frequently support my own conclusions as much as his. This goes particularly for "some fundamental historical facts that have unfortunately escaped the author's attention." They have indeed escaped me. But they rarely contradict me. Rather they fill in some powerful details in a tableau I have sketched in more sweeping terms.

1. How the Poor Aided and Still Aid the Rich

His figures show, for example, how the poor countries have always helped the rich rather than the rich the poor. This is one of my very reasons for suggesting that the statesmen of the poor are double fools for seeking continued links with the rich. Professor Thorne thus merely emphasizes my point when he demonstrates by the example of the Canadian-British Guianan relationship that, what is so often passed off as aid, amounts even today under a more disarming name not to aid but to continued exploitation of the assisted by their assisters, who are prevented from doing otherwise not by malevolence but by their huge headstart.

In view of precisely this sort of experience, my question now is: Should one go on requesting or accepting aid which, however benign its intent, brings more benefits to the giver than the recipient? Or should one, what seems to me the more logical alternative, seek Development *Without* Aid. I may be wrong, but at least one of the post-war leaders of the underdeveloped world whose motives were rarely doubted by the others, the late President Sukarno of Indonesia, stumbled on the same idea when, on January 8, 1965, he told both the United States and the United Nations: "Go to hell with your aid . . . Now we dare face all consequences. Let us face all difficulties. Only through overcoming difficulties can we become a great nation . . . and march onward, ever onward, never retreat." Now, while I feel that Sukarno's underlying jingoistic megalomania was not half as attractive as his army of aid-consuming girl friends, I was delighted with his belated insight and, in fact, was giving thought to retitling my volume: "To Hell With Aid."

I have therefore no dispute with Professor Thorne when he says: "The colonies and former colonies do not really receive 'lavish aid'," though some of them do, even in the critical eye of the Soviet Union. Thus, according to a January 1965 report of the United Nations *Economic Commission for Latin America,* Russia and her satellites have between 1959 and 1963 assisted or, as I prefer to put it, burdened a Cuba, trying to get on its own feet, with no less than $700 million in grants, credits and other aid. I would call this rather lavish even if one ignores the additional $1 billion in military assistance, the effect of which must inevitably be that Cuba will be less socialized than militarized; and less Cubanized than, as is the fate of any large-scale recipient of foreign equipment, internationally standardized and alienized— a fine achievement for Fidel Castro, a social reformer and proud nationalist leader who, defying all academic opinion, started out by staging *unaided* a revolution so spectacular that he would have become the Achilles of the Americas had he had the good fortune to be assassinated on the day he entered Havana.

However, as I said, I have basically no dispute with Professor Thorne when he suggests that the underdeveloped countries do not really *receive* lavish aid. My point in challenging the horse-sense of their leaders was that they *ask* for it. For as Professor Thorne himself has so convincingly shown, they are thereby unwittingly helping the exploiters of the past to perpetuate the plunder of their lands by signing, in the guise of guilt-absolving aid agreements, unprofitable profit-splitting arrangements that contribute little to their own development.

2. Soft Loans Versus Aid

Nor do these leaders emerge in a more favourable light if one accepts Professor Thorne's interpretation that the aid they receive or solicit is not only far from lavish, but is in the nature of soft loans which cannot properly be classified as aid in the first place. For though repayable on favourable terms, they are still repayable, as Bassanio's loan was to Shylock.

I wish I could go along with this interpretation. However, repayable or not, soft loan or hard, the recipient of a loan asks for it obviously in the conviction that he cannot achieve his ends without it. So even a loan is aid, and the measure of its aid is expressed not by the small differential between hard and soft rates of interest but by the magnitude of the principal.

There is, moreover, another element emphasizing the aid-character of loans received from rich foreign governments. This is the chance that they may never be reclaimed, not so much because the aided country may be unable to render, as because the granting country may in the end be unable to accept, repayments, as is the case when too many similar repayments fall due at the same time as a result of an earlier flood of similar grants. This is why after World War I only Finland was permitted by the United States to play the role of the only honest aid recipient amongst the allies, and deliver in a regularly photographed ceremony on the steps of the Washington Treasury her annual repayment quota—because it was a pittance. The rest of Europe was forced into default not because it could not have paid, but because of the inability of a prosperous America to absorb Europe's enormous repayment sums without the danger of thereby disrupting its own economy. This is why, fifty years earlier, Bismarck resolved that, next time he won a war, he would demand of the defeated enemy, not to pay, but to *accept* indemnities. For he had just learned the bitter lesson that, by absorbing instead of refusing the immense French reparation payments after 1871, the rich economy of victorious Germany had been pushed into depression while defeated France had been given the chance of working herself into prosperity.

So when the leaders of the underdeveloped countries ask "merely" for loans, they may in the end find themselves forced to accept them as gifts, if for no other reason than to help the giver out of his *embarras de richesses*. This would of course be a welcome windfall in the case of consumer loans. But in the case of development loans, relief from repayment obligations, as depression-struck Europe found out in the twenties, means at once a curtailment of the very productive power and subsequent trading potential the loan was presumed to have created.

Hence, whether loans stay loans or turn into gifts, I can see little practical purpose in making a distinction between the two. Either of them is desired as a form of aid, for nobody not wanting aid would ask for either; and both tend to help the parties involved in proportion to their stage of development, bringing in spite of the best of intentions more benefits to the donor than the recipient, to the rich than the poor, to the advanced than the retarded, just as an equal thrust imparted to bodies moving at different speeds will accelerate the faster more than the slower with the result of widening the gap between them instead of reducing it.

But whatever one may make of the distinction between soft loans and gifts, my primary argument against large-scale aid in any form, under any name, on any ground, even if it *should* contribute to the material advance of the recipient, is still that the introduction of alien tools, created in response to alien environment by an alien mind, cannot but alienize a nation from its own identity. And I am not alone in this idea. It is shared by Karl

Marx, who is so venerated in emerging nations that they think it unnecessary to acquaint themselves with this central dogma. This is that historic action and historic development are determined not by religions, great leaders, economic systems, or ideologies— all opiates for the people, administered for the painless extraction of sacrifice; they are determined by the *mode of production;* by the ways and tools with which we earn our living. Tools alien to our experience alienize us, which is of course a perfectly proper aim for reviled international capitalists or not so reviled internationalizing communists, but hardly for the nationalist leaders of nascent nations trying to shape for their peoples a mode of life setting them apart and making them distinguishable from all others. And the only way of shaping a nationally distinct mode of life is the hard way. As Sukarno said when denouncing all foreign aid: "Only through overcoming difficulties" can a nation become great, and find its soul for that matter.

3.   Favourable Terms of Trade Versus Aid

What applies to soft loans applies also to the other alternative which the statesmen of underdeveloped countries are said to prefer to aid: more favourable terms of trade. For similar to soft loans, these too are not an alternative to, but merely a different form of, aid. They are solicited because the underdeveloped countries feel too weak to develop *unaided* in the face of terms of trade imposed by the interplay of the giant amoral forces dominating the international markets not because they are bad[1] but because they are strong. So they ask these amoral giants to be good enough to accord them terms that would enable them to

[1] As Gunnar Myrdal writes in *Rich Lands And Poor*: "In judging the economic results of colonialism and foreign domination, I think it would contribute to avoiding an irrational heightening of the resentments" of the underdeveloped nations "if the main thesis of this book were constantly borne in mind: namely, that because of circular causation a tendency toward inequality is inherent in the unhampered play of the market forces, and particularly so when the general level of economic development is low. Nationally, once a country has reached a higher average level of development, this tendency will be offset by the spread effect of expansionary momentum, and national integration policies. Internationally, . . . the spread effects are much weaker and the cumulative process will more easily go in the direction of inequality if the forces in the market are given free play." (*Op. cit.* p. 56).

rise above the shadows cast by their excessive strength.

All this might make sense if countries were underdeveloped because they suffer from unfavourable terms of trade. But it is the other way round. They suffer from unfavourable terms of trade because they are underdeveloped. They are weak in trade because they are weak in structure, and they will no more get stronger by being granted terms that are not the cause but the consequence of strength than a boy will get adult by being put into grown-up pants. On the contrary!

The most logical way for underdeveloped countries of escaping the impeding effect of unfavourable terms of trade, it would seem to me, is therefore to seek redress in the opposite direction: overcome their handicap not by lengthening their bodies but by shortening their pants, by asking not for better but for less trade, concentrating not on bargain buying, but on producing what cannot be had at a bargain themselves; insisting not on further expanding but on shrinking their lopsided overdeveloped export sector, and applying the resources thus released to the building up of a distortion-resistant consumption-oriented industry for the home market instead.

In short, the alternative I propose is: to aim at balanced growth by achieving physical development first, and cross the bridge of international trade only when the overspill from a differently structured, wholesomely diversified domestic production reaches it. Then the *terms of trade* will automatically keep at all points their proper level with a country's rising natural *power to trade,* without the need of soliciting support. For, once trade is resumed *after* physical development is achieved rather than *for* the achievement of physical development, the imported manufactured goods will no longer consist of primary essentials that must be acquired at any cost and can be paid for only through either the sacrifice of consumption or the aid of favourable terms of trade, but of luxuries payable out of the overspill created by increased efficiency in production. This is admittedly in its first phases a somewhat tougher alternative. But I feel sure I do not need to quote Sukarno's twice quoted *Ode on Hardship* a third time.

If this natural growth sequence in which trade is the result rather than the tool of progress is reversed, and trade is emphasized *before* full physical development is achieved, economic advance is not only *not* assisted. Like the walk of a boy impeded by the flapping of grown-up pants, it becomes twice as hard. In fact, it was precisely this that caused the retardation of colonial economies in the first place. Being right from the start built up for trade, of trade, by trade; and benefiting from a premature inclusion in the immensity of free imperial and world markets; the very laws of absolute and comparative advantage so dear to propagandists of international specialization operated only for those with a head start, and against those starting with a lag.[1] For they so favoured the lopsided overdevelopment of a few profitable export crops such as coffee, cotton, or "bitter" sugar that, even if no fruit trees had been chopped down, no resources would have been left for diversifying the economy into other areas which were vital to domestic consumption and balanced growth, but detrimental to profitable foreign trade.

Retardation through trade has therefore been the inevitable fate of every backward region entertaining commercial relations with the superior market forces of advanced countries since antiquity. Petronius gives us a picture of this when he tells us in the introductory poem to his *Satyricon* how "here the Numidians, there the Seres, wove for the Roman new fleeces, and for him the Arab tribes plundered their steppes."[2] And Professor Thorne has himself underlined this distortion-generating relationship by quoting from Cunningham to the effect that traders in the Southern and West Indian Colonies "were not specially concerned to foster communities which should be self-sufficing; they preferred that the planters should manage their estates with a view to the requirement of outside markets." Indeed, so disastrous was the consequence of their trade fixation, fuelled, as it is today, by an

---

[1] The same idea, that trade between regions and countries of unequal development stage tends to advance the advanced and retard the retarded, is the central theme of Gunnar Myrdal's "theory of circular and cumulative causation", brilliantly developed in his book *Rich Lands and Poor*. Again and again he stresses that the "main theme" he wants "to convey is that the play of the forces of the market normally tends to increase, rather than to decrease, the inequalities between regions," and that "market forces will tend cumulatively to accentuate international inequalities" (*Op. cit.*, p. 26 and p. 55).

[2] *Daily Life in Ancient Rome*. By Jerome Carcopino. Peregrine Books, Y23, p. 1948.

airtight body of received economic doctrine, that, as Professor Thorne continues to quote, Virginia ran the risk of not even providing her food supply from her rich soil, and Charles I "feared that the future of the territory was being sacrificed to the immediate gain of the planters," even as many of the newly liberated countries of today run the risk of being sacrificed to the instant prestige requirements of their trade-oriented liberators in search not of private gain, which would at least benefit somebody, but of sterile public pedestals for their own monuments, which serve nobody.

4. Development Through Trade

This does not mean that underdeveloped countries can not also develop with the help of favourable terms of trade. What it means is that, contrary to what Professor Thorne implies, trading favours must be classified as aid in the same sense as soft loans. And this being the case, they will of necessity have the same alienizing effect on countries struggling for their identity as any other kind of large-scale aid.

But this is not all. Gearing an economy thus assisted from the outset to the opportunities of the external rather than the domestic market, the resulting industrial diversification is likely to become as lopsided as the preceding specialization. For trade-oriented development tends to do with a whole range of production areas what colonial development had done only with a few. Adding artificial to natural market advantages, it overdevelops them. Instead of inducing inner-directed diversification, it diversifies the other-directed export sector, thereby aggravating the distortion factor by putting even more rather than less of the economy at the mercy of extraneous decision makers.

Moreover, trying to finance a rise in domestic living standards through the indirect means of trading profits rather than by tackling it head-on through the evolution of a production pattern directly related to it, such a development runs into a number of other difficulties. First, there is the inevitable seepage into inefficiency and corruption that tends to reduce the advantage that might otherwise be gained from roundabout approaches. Secondly, the fruit of roundabout approaches invariably registers first on the radar screen of statistics. And living standard improvements achieved through the intermediary of trade rather than direct production may look considerably more impressive in figures on which the politicians feed, than in terms of the substance that filters down to the supper table of the man who lives on rice and beans. As the youth complained: "According to statistics, there are 2.7 women to every man—and I have none." And thirdly, the most pressing target of every economic development is to raise first of all the standards of those living at the lowest levels. But the world of international trade is so complex, and needs such a battery of experts and executive talent which, moreover, not yet being available at home, must be imported at high salaries from abroad, that the first rewards must of course go to the traders, the shippers, the bankers, the brokers, the contact men, the advisers, the economists, the statisticians, the lawyers, the educators, the bureaucracy, while it may take a generation before the trading profits are able to make a dent in the slums. In other words, development through trade reverses the hierarchy of concern, placing those who should be the prime beneficiaries of progress last.[1]

Still, I grant, in the end countries aided by favourable terms of trade can, at a somewhat slower pace but with an earlier chance of gratifying the first reapers of profit, achieve the same high level of development through an economy diversified for international trade, as one that has diversified for the nearer home market and confines trade to its overspill. But unlike the latter, and this is my principal reproach to the nation builders of our time from a strictly political point of view, theirs will be an economy thriving, yes; but thriving in abject dependence on markets beyond their boundaries, and on forces beyond their control. Is this all their leaders can think of? Replace political with economic dependence? And behave not much differently from those colonial planters, cited by Professor Thorne not exactly as models of deportment, who, rather than "foster communities which should be self-sufficing," preferred to "manage their estates with a view to the requirement of outside markets"? I should have thought they would have found more charm in the philosophy of *Development*

[1] See the Casteñeda-Herrero study in *Revista de Ciencias Sociales,* referred to in footnote 1 on p. 116.

Without Aid or, for that matter, in Thomas Aquinas who, in his *Government of Rulers* (11, 3), wrote: "The higher a thing is, the more self-sufficient it is; since whatever needs another's help is by that fact inferior. But that city is more fully self-sufficient, which the surrounding country supplies with all its vital needs, than is another which must obtain these supplies by trade."

5. Development by Common Market

Since Professor Thorne has himself made the point that the leaders of underdeveloped countries prefer to develop with the help of favourable terms of trade, he will agree with me that favourable terms of trade make sense only for those who are interested in foreign trade. He will also agree that those interested in foreign trade will try to secure foreign markets. And he will agree that the best way of securing foreign markets is for trading partners of moderate domestic markets to band together in the creation of a treaty-secured *common* market which fuses their territories economically while leaving their political status unaffected. This is why I wrote on the very first page of *Development Without Aid* that "there is a consensus of opinion that all that is needed for speedy progress is banding together."

Professor Thorne wonders about my "source of information that permits such a definite statement on such an extremely wide generalization," and suggests that "certainly the many so-called 'development plans' of the underdeveloped countries do not support the affirmation. . . . Even in the Central American countries, where a common market is already a reality and is already stimulating growth, the plans seldom include more than a passing reference to the common market. The 'plans' are much more preoccupied with the well-known types of programmes for inducing growth."

Granted. But is there not a vast difference between growth programmes stimulated by limited domestic markets and those responding to the stimulus of much larger common markets? Though it may not be stressed, without the background of Puerto Rico's common market with the United States, the island's phenomenal hotel development would have spent itself in the construction of a few guest houses. Similarly if, as Professor

Thorne says, the Central American common market is already stimulating growth, it is obvious that the local growth programmes of its member states must already have assumed a radically different shape from what they would have been without it, even if they mention the cause responsible for the change with no more than a "passing reference." And the same seems to apply to the "well-known types" of growth-inducing programmes in the rest of the Caribbean, none of which, I admit, contains even a passing reference to the prospect of a common market. Yet, the eminently official, though now in the process of dying, *Caribbean Organization,* which annually publishes both a collection of all development plans of the countries served by it, and a volume on *Intra-Caribbean Trade Statistics,* does so for the specific purpose of preparing the ground for their adjustment to a future common market.

The compilations of the *Caribbean Organization* together with the comments of their officers are one of my sources from which I have drawn my "generalization." Another is a study by Carlos E. Chardon, exploring the possibility of a Puerto Rican common market with the Dominican Republic, published in 1962 by the official Government Development Bank of Puerto Rico under the title: *Datos que Sugieren la Integracion de Una Parte de la Region del Caribe: La Republica Dominicana y Puerto Rico.* A third is my own annotated common market documentation compiled in two years of work for the Carnegie Endowment for International Peace, and so voluminous (6,000—six thousand—pages) that the list of document titles together with my bibliography alone fills a 70-page appendix to Jacob Viner's *The Customs Union Issue* (New York: Carnegie Endowment for International Peace, 1950, pp. 141-211).

It is particularly this compilation which informed me that underdeveloped Latin America, as the most enthusiastic student of the German *Zollverein* long before the European Economic Community was even conceived, has been responsible for a veritable avalanche of unofficial *and* official projects for the creation of similar economic unions on a regional, continental, and even hemispheric basis. Some of them were included in the preambles to a number of formal treaties such as between Argentina and Brazil (1941), Argentina, Chile, and Paraguay (1943), Argentina and Bolivia (1947). Others led to agreements such as the Quito Charter of 1948, committing Colombia, Ecuador, Panama, and Venezuela to the establishment of the *Gran Colombia Economic and Customs Union;* and still others, to agreements actually establishing such unions as the treaty of 1958 among Honduras, Guatemala, El Salvador, Nicaragua, Costa Rica; and the speed-up treaty of 1960 among Honduras, Guatemala, and El Salvador. And a similarly buzzing treaty activity has characterized Africa, one of the more publicized ones establishing a common market among the formerly "united" Arab republics having been signed in 1964.[1]

And last, there is the unending string of conferences where the statesmen, experts, and advisors of underdeveloped countries "band together" to discover how they might speed up their development by common planning within the larger context *of* their combined resources. Why otherwise should they get together? For staying apart? In fact, while I was writing the first chapters of *Development Without Aid* (hence the location of my criticized "consensus" remark on its very first page), a Carribbean Conference, attended by such international luminaries as Professor Tinbergen, the first winner of the Nobel Prize in Economics, sat assembled in the sumptuous lounges of Puerto Rico's Condado Beach Hotel; and though it is true that the subject of a common market was not even with a passing reference included in the official agenda, it permeated each and every one of its discussions. It is as with America's pursuit of happiness. It is mentioned in the founding documents with no more than a single phrase. Yet, is there anything permeating American life more than exactly this?

So I feel I must stick to my "extremely wide generalization," just as the top of an iceberg must stick to its submerged part of which it is but a small projection into visibility. This does, however, not mean that my criticism of the seeming consensus of underdeveloped countries in trying to speed their advance by co-ordinating their economies implies that common markets may

[1] For further information indicating the extraordinary popularity of the idea of developing by means of common markets, see the author's *Customs Unions—a Tool of Peace,* Washington, Foundation for Foreign Affairs, 1949; "The History of the Common Market," in *Journal of Economic History,* September 1960; and *Wales and The Common Market,* by Gwynfor Evans, based in part on the author's material.

not under given historic circumstances make sense. They do. When the German states joined in their *Zollverein,* eye witness accounts, (quoted earlier in footnote 1, on p. 35), tell us of the justified joy with which the trading world greeted the abolition of customs barriers at the opening hour of the year 1834. "Long trains of wagons stood at the high roads, which till then had been cut by tax barriers. At the stroke of midnight, every turnpike was thrown open, and amid cheers the wagons hastened over the boundaries, which they could henceforth cross in freedom. Everyone felt a great objective had been obtained."

As this eye witness account suggests, here the common market *did* make sense because the prospective members had *already* reached such a high level of independent growth that the overspill from their consequently balanced, mature, diversified, consumption-oriented domestic production had long begun to fill the wagons joyfully waiting on *both* sides of the boundaries for the signal that brought them freedom of movement. But imagine the joyful scenes of long trains of cars bursting across the boundaries after the elimination of customs barriers separating, let us say, Bolivia and Brazil! Their islands of economic activity are still so few and far apart, and their thinly spread populations as yet so far beyond each other's horizon, that their roads still barely touch. As a result, in contrast to the *Zollverein,* the hour ushering in their union would witness neither traders, nor wagons, nor overspill surging across solitary boundaries that separate not because of political obstruction but because of emptiness as well as geopgraphic and economic distances. Any effort to bind them together just for the sake of producing links before their systems even touch would require the wasteful construction of such a huge transportation and communication network that this alone would throw back the chance of developing a balanced production economy from the ground by decades.

Since togetherness, exchange, common action stunt if pushed before their time, while arising spontaneously upon touch, union in common markets or even much looser trade associations can, as I suggested, have no more sense for those not yet fully developed than union in marriage. Instead of offering possibilities to the present, it tends to retard the future by providing a premature chance for trying, when neither strength nor wisdom is as yet proportionate to desire.[1]

6. *Development in the Perspective of History: The United States*

Nothing of the foregoing means that I challenge the idea that trade and market involvements may not be sources of added riches, as I have tried to show by referring to the example of the *Zollverein*. What I challenge is the idea that such international involvements are good for all development stages, and particularly, that arrangements linking the retarded with the more advanced will benefit the retarded. Historically, links of this kind have always produced the opposite results. They have led to polarization, advancing the advanced, and increasing the exploitation-inviting gap of retardation still further. I have illustrated this by the example not only of a number of colony-motherland relationships but also of such closer ties between unequal partners as the unions between England and Wales, England and Scotland, Italy and Calabria, Russia and Siberia, France and Brittany (p. 22). Soviet textbooks have gone one better by detecting imperialist exploitation even in the relationships existing between a naturally dominant metropolis such as Moscow, or Havana for that matter, and its belt of invariably more retarded rural communities surrounding it.[1] And by adding to my own illustrations the examples of a number of "empire histories", Professor Thorne has once again, I venture to say, not weakened but rather strengthened my case with some excellent supplementary historic evidence that had indeed escaped my attention.

[1] Gunnar Myrdal (*op. cit.*, p. 28) again provides excellent examples for this. See my quotation in footnote 2 of page 22.

[1] See N. N. Baransky. *Economic Geography of the Soviet Union.* Moscow 1956, where he writes on p. 10: "Just as tsarist Russia was a tributary of Western capitalism, within Russia herself the colonial outlying regions were tributaries of the metropolis, i.e., of the central part of the country located around Moscow,"—which, of course, they are still today. As a result of a similar tributary relationship, the canton of Basel split in 1833 into the now independent Swiss half-cantons of *Basel-City* and *Basel-land*, after the rural districts revolted against the oppressive rule of urban trade guilds. See author's *The Breakdown of Nations,* New York: Rinehart 1957.

It is because of this retarding and distorting effect of premature trade involvements that the underdeveloped countries of the past, unlike those of our own time, have always set out on their road to development not by extending but by contracting their available foreign markets. Instead of trade facilities, they demanded protection; protection not *of* their commercial involvements, but *from* commercial involvements, particularly with countries more advanced than themselves. Thus the young United States considered it essential for her development to add, after forty years of futile struggle, commercial to her political boundaries, and to withdraw after 1812 behind the protection of "economic nationalism" and "tariffs of abomination,"—a policy which was viewed by both the slave-owning defenders of free trade in the South and the then dominant classical *laissez-faire* school of advanced economists across the seas with the same suspicion of reactionary implication with which the contemporary establishment of economists view my idea that similar policies of protective isolation might make sense for countries finding themselves today in similar stages of underdevelopment.

I grant that, by the standards of the then "received" doctrine, America's "economic nationalism" was in its time theoretically all wrong. But what miracles it produced in practical "bootstrap" growth as compared with the "right" ideas that might have kept them bottled up in monographs, had not the leaders of the day had the courage to prepare their giant leaps forward by the "reactionary" method of first taking a few steps back. They had been taught by bitter experience that, if countries are to gain by trade, they must already have reached a high degree of balanced industrial diversification in their own right which, satisfying their basic needs in depth, will then automatically yield the margin of wealth-*adding* surplus in which trade becomes both possible and profitable *without* the danger of distorting the domestic economy. If, on the other hand, they were submerged in the ocean of free markets too soon, they had learned that no degree of political independence could avert their continued status as economic colonies. For the very laws of comparative advantage would condemn them to unfavourable terms of trade becoming the more unfavourable the greater the trade, and the more retarding the wider the resulting discrepancy in head start between the trading partners.

What corrected the initial economic distortion of the young United States and subsequently protected it from the distortion-aggravating effect of neo-colonialism, of which contemporary former colonies complain so much, was therefore not independence but their shift from outward-looking trading to inward-looking diversified self-sufficiency. And what permitted right from the beginning the distortion-averting diversification of Austria, France, Holland, Liechtenstein, and the mass of German and Italian states, which Professor Thorne mentions in favourable contrast to the helpless lopsidedness of colonial development, is the same thing. It was not their independence—an economically irrelevant condition in the interdependent world of trade. Nor was it the volume of their *future* trade. It was their *original* policy of a largely tradeless self-sufficiency, which their leaders dared to adopt on the strength of simple native rather than of hallowed imported advice. Finding its doctrinal expression in such well-known classics as Philip von Hornick's *Oesterreich Ueber Alles Wenn es nur Will,* or Antoine de Montchrétien's *Traicté de l' OEconomie Politique,* which is incidentally the first volume said to contain the term "political economy," its central dogma of proud self-sufficiency was perhaps best summarized by the latter's appeal to the King of France: *"Faites-nous donc jouissance du fruict de nostre industrie; c'est a dire, rendez-nous á nous mesmes."*[1] Give us back to ourselves!

7. *Example of Athens*

Historically we therefore rarely find nations owing their original wealth to trade. Many of them may have sprung into prominence only after they had reached a prosperous trading status. But they too had to pass through a prior phase of less publicized bootstrap growth in inner-directed isolation. As Walter Bagehot said: "All the great nations have been prepared in privacy and in secret. They have been composed away from all distraction",[2] not by orating before the United Nations.

1 Alexander Gray. *Development of Economic Doctrine.* New York: John Wiley, 1961, p. 83 (Quoted from 1889 reprint by Funck-Brentano, p. 73).

2 Quoted by Arnold J. Toynbee, *A Study of History.* New York: Oxford University Press, 1947, p. 224.

This is particularly true also of ancient Athens, though Professor Thorne is of course as always quite correct when he writes that "the Athenian culture in the Golden Age of Greece lay upon what was for that period a sound economic foundation, and that a large part of this foundation consisted of a successful trade." But what he overlooks is that the golden Pericleian Age of trading did not burst full-blown out of the head of Zeus. It was preceded by the silver Peisistratean Age of building up and diversifying domestic production for its own needs. Without it the subsequent mercantile Pericleian Age would have been as unthinkable as the second stage of a space rocket is without the first. Pericles traded in fruit. But, as I suggested in *Development Without Aid,* it was Peisistratus who planted the trees, and built much of the golden Acropolis in addition. So there were two Athens, and the one I have held up as example for the stage which contemporary underdeveloped countries must duplicate if they are to reap Pericleian gold, is the first, not the more publicized second. The lovely butterfly takes off on wings only after it has been a lowly caterpillar, and only *because* it has been a caterpillar fulfilling its preparatory mission without any thought of adjusting its activities to a future of winged existence that is the more assured the more it lives as an inner-directed caterpillar, not as an air-oriented ground worm with butterfly ambitions.

This indispensable two-stage, caterpillar-butterfly, character of all economic development would have been clearer, had not economic scholarship consistently confused the inward-looking bootstrap stage of industrialization and the outward-looking mercantile phase of trading, which logically and historically always followed one another, by lumping the dominant guidelines of both together under the hodge-podge term of *mercantilism.*

This could never have happened to a categorizer such as Aristotle. But one can understand why it did happen for a variety of reasons. In the first place, like the various grades in a one-room rural school, the two stages invariably existed side by side, Austria moving in at the bottom, while England was already halfway up. Secondly, the line dividing the second stage from the first, out of which it insensibly evolved in an uninterrupted sequence of years, seemed over the distance of centuries frequently so narrow to modern observers that, like the light from far-away twin stars, the information emanating from the first got all too easily entwined in the denser information received from the more documented, more glamorized, and more adventuresome second phase. Thirdly, contemporary authors describing the second stage in one set of countries, such as Thomas Mun (1571-1641) in England, were often the contemporaries of authors such as Antoine de Monchrétien (1576-1621) witnessing and describing the first stage in another set of countries such as France. And lastly, with both stages of economic development forming part of the undivided larger political process of nation building, they were inevitably characterized by a number of common *political* features such as what Alexander Gray calls a pervasive socialist "policy of ubiquitous and perpetual government activity" (op. cit., pp. 77-78), which increased the impression that the two *economic* stages must also have been one and the same.

Yet, all the time the term *cameralism* might have led to a clear distinction between the two, had not the scholars used it as a name for describing merely a central European variant of mercantilism rather than the stage that invariably preceded it even in the countries whose authors took to their pen only during the more intriguing and complex later phase when all their energies were required for the intellectual dismantlement of the by then obsolete concepts inherited from the earlier period.

8. *The Puerto Rican Lesson*

But there is no need for going back to either ancient Athens or 17th-Century cameralism-mercantilism to appreciate the two-stage caterpillar-butterfly character of all economic development, as well as the fact that, brief as the span between the two stages may be, they must always follow each other rather than be attempted simultaneously, if crippling distortions are to be avoided. All we need do is look from our windows at contemporary Puerto Rico which started on its rise not by mercantilistically improving its terms of trade, but first of all by concentrating on developing and diversifying its industry in its famous cameralist monly known. Only after this was well on its way could it think of entering on its second, mercantilist, stage, symbolized by the appointment in 1959 of our distinguished colleague Dr. Carlos Lastra as her first Secretary of Commerce. Ten years earlier, the suggestion of a Department of Commerce would have been considered reckless, and would have met with the question: "What should we sell besides our 'bitter' sugar and the opiate of rum? More of it?" The answer with regard to these mainstays of trade was: less of it!—always in the awareness that the best way of reducing the unwelcome consequences of a thing is not by increasing but by proportionately reducing it.

By this I do not wish to say that, yielding to the irresistible temptation of the huge American market, Puerto Rico's "cameralist" *Operation Bootstrap*—like most of the "well-known types of programmes for inducing growth" in the rest of the Caribbean countries—was not also out of tune with a harmonious progress towards less a prosperous than a *securely* prosperous future. Its achievement was spectacular! But gearing its industrialization right from the beginning to production for a future external rather than a domestic market, to the cycle-ridden uncertainties of foreign trade rather than the predictable security of an increasingly sophisticated internal consumption, the Puerto Rican experiment will, I am afraid, in the end only prove that a diversified economy can be as lopsided as a narrowly specialized one; and that a foreign market-oriented industry is as dependent on alien whims as a colonial one.

So I am aware that, as in so many other instances, the Puerto Rican example is not always the best to illustrate the most logical processes of economic growth. It illustrates the two-stage nature of development. And it is an excellent example for showing the speed with which a country of limited size can push economic growth under local leadership if the two stages are arranged in proper sequence. But it also shows what happens when, in spite of the proper time sequence, the different purposes of the two stages get mixed up, and the cameralist caterpillar phase becomes prematurely dominated by the mercantilist dream of a winged butterfly existence.

For now that Puerto Rico has reached the beginnings of her butterfly stage, she finds herself producing so many wings that not even the enormous American market seems to offer enough space to satisfy their need for constant exercise in soaring commercial flight. Hence her paradoxical attempt to create, while still partly underdeveloped, a Caribbean market empire of her own, in the hope of unloading on less advanced communities a growing overspill she cannot absorb locally since it has not been adjusted to domestic consumption. And the situation is even more paradoxical if one considers that, though her own market is not large enough to absorb her overspill in the airy butterfly amenities she does not consume, she constitutes at the same time one of the most lucrative markets for overspill generated outside Puerto Rico in the more earthly and more essential caterpillar commodities she has ceased to produce.[1]

And the same is true of other countries trying to imitate the Puerto Rican example without the saving grace of a political association with an America compelled on family grounds to underwrite the deficit and unfavourable trade conditions resulting from misdirected development. It makes no difference whether the official programmes of these countries are, as Professor Thorne has pointed out, merely of the orthodox growth-inducing variety that make nary a mention of a future of trade. For none of these programmes, as far as I can see from my admittedly much less documented perspective, can succeed without the insurance of a foreign sales volume exceeding by far the proportions of a legitimate overspill.[2]

I do not think I need figures to back this up, when I learn in approximations that Ceylon's new steel mill is so productive that

[1] Puerto Rico is second only to Canada as the largest market for U.S. goods in the Americas, and occupies fifth place in the entire world. According to the Puerto Rican Planning Board (*Ingreso y Producto*, 1959, 1957-1960, A-85), she had to import in 1960 80% of all her clothing and accessories; 94.4% of her tobacco products; 91.9% of personal care; 64.7% of meat; 70.8% of all goods connected with household operations; 78.1% of transportation commodities; 48.5% of food; and a grand total of 58.4% of all goods consumed.

[2] By an economically legitimate overspill I understand one composed of the sum of individually modest surpluses generated in a wide range of consumption-oriented diversified economic activities as a result of natural advantages and technical efficiency. This presupposes a high degree of self-sufficiency amounting to perhaps 80% or 85%, so that the economy can survive without deep-reaching dislocation due to external forces over which it has no control.

it is able to fill all domestic needs in six weeks (or is it twelve?). What will it produce the rest of the year? Maoist revolutionaries? Reactionary visionaries preaching a return to nature? Obviously the only way of keeping it busy is for Ceylon to band together with other less developed "steel colonies" until a market empire is created large enough to utilize also the rest of her productive capacity in respect of a commodity whose overspill is anything but economically legitimate, considering that it is not the incidental residual product of natural advantage and technical efficiency but a weapon shaped by purposeful planning in anticipation of mercantile conquest.

It shows that, contrary to Marx, the search for external markets seems to commit not only profit-seeking capitalism to a policy of imperialist expansion. *Any* external-market seeking economic philosophy is driven along the same path. For it too sees its only hope of profitably unloading its system-conditioned surpluses—which cannot be absorbed domestically, either by matured capitalism because of its lopsided distribution pattern or by a directed growth economy because of its lopsided production and market structure—by selling them in less advanced regions. As a result, what it nurtures is the same kind of vested interest in the latter's continued retardation as capitalism. Only markets of equal advance lose their imperialist incentives and, again contrary to Marx, do so even under capitalism.

However, this was not really the point I meant to make when citing Puerto Rico as an example at this juncture of the argument. Here I meant to demonstrate the historic sequence in which bootstrap (industrialization) and mercantile phases of development must *follow* each other even under such favoured conditions as Puerto Rico's (which tend to obscure the unwholesome effects of premature market orientation), and even in our own time (which is otherwise characterized by its ability to speed up all processes). This is the more important as, looking back into the dimness of the past, the span of years separating the two *successive* development phases appears so thin as to become almost invisible, thus giving rise to the understandable yet unhistoric illusion that a state such as Athens owed its prosperity to Pericleian trade. A flowering margin of it, yes. But its foundation it owed to the hardship of prior labour, undertaken in unpublicized seclusion, "away from all distraction," by Pelsistratus a hundred years earlier.

9. Aid as Compensation for Past Sins

So far I have challenged the economic horsesense of development of trade, by trade, for trade, on the ground that what drains the resources of retarded countries is not the *type* but the *fact* of links tying them to more advanced countries. Hence my suggestion to cut the links altogether at first and develop without aid, rather than merely change the type of links by turning an imperial command relationship into a contractual one; substituting foreign bankers for foreign soldiers and foreign-trained technicians for foreign-trained bureaucrats, all drinking from the same academic wells.

But economic reasons are not the only ones which Professor Thorne has advanced in defence of the leaders of underdeveloped countries. He also defends them on moral grounds when he writes: "They know well that there is no possibility of their people ever being compensated fully for the forced contributions made by generations of their sweated and bullied ancestors to the then poor but now rich developed countries"; and concludes that there is therefore no reason why they should consider it "undignified to try to reduce the present drain of their poor countries' resources to the developed countries, as far as they can, through 'aid' or soft loans."

Though Professor Thorne introduces the improper-conduct and guilt—implying concepts of dignity and compensation in only a single passing reference, I feel this shift from the economic to the moral aspects of the argument for assisted development merits a more extensive discussion. For aside from going to the very heart of the matter, it also touches on the one point in which I disagree with my friend in depth. The reasons for this are the following:

In the first place, as I have tried to show from the beginning, large-scale aid in any form—gifts, soft loans, favourable terms of trade—alienizes, disrupts, distorts. It makes no difference whether such aid is morally justified or not. It still corrupts the country extracting it.

Secondly, if aid is used rationally rather than morally or emotionally, its purpose must be development, which stimulates effort, not compensation for past sins, which lulls it. And not only do compensation payments lull effort. They tend at the same time to plant the seed for the commission of future sins considering that those called upon to render compensation have in all likelihood little in common with the generation of original sinners. But having to pay for what they have not done, is it not reasonable that—like the factotum in Kurt Goetz's play *Dr. med. Hiob Praetorius*—they should ultimately wish to partake a little in the joy of committing the sins for which they are made responsible anyway? While punishment often follows prior crime, crime also often follows prior punishment.

Thirdly, the exploiters of colonies have never been the nations but the impersonal machinery of the state, and the state does not distinguish between people at home and people in the colonies. It distinguishes between the ruling class, the elite, the establishment on the one hand, and the indiscriminate mass of the ruled, the exploited, on the other. The villain oppressing colonial peoples was therefore the imperial state, not the imperial people, which was as much the victim of the rulers, if the much venerated Karl Marx was right, as the colonials. And since the victims of past exploitation have in the meantime assumed control of the machinery of the state not only in the former colonies but also in many of the former homelands, any retributive aid extracted by the descendants of one set of victims would hit the descendants not of the now subdued, powerless, and largely expropriated former exploiters, but of another set of victims—the previously universally abused working class.

This is quite aside from my conviction, which I feel sure is shared by Professor Thorne, that guilt does not transmit itself from ancestor to descendant. As a descendant of the Austro-Hungarian empire, I feel no guilt complex whatsoever for what Francis Joseph, assisted by the Austrian, Czech, Hungarian, Galician, Croat, Slovak, Slovene, etc., establishment, may have meted out to his subject peoples, and if any citizen of the "succession" states should claim retribution from me, my reaction would not be understanding compliance but an offer of collaboration with anyone planning their renewed oppression. And I am sure our colleague Fuat Andic, a descendant of the ferocious Turkish empire, now, like myself, reduced to earning a meagre living by teaching instead of practicing economics, will feel the same. All of us are guilty enough in our own right to be senselessly burdened with the sins of our fathers or, still worse, with the impersonal sins of the state and of politico-economic systems over which no one except the existing ruling elite has power.

Fourthly, even if there were such a thing as collective guilt, which the Western Allies of the last two wars attributed to the Germans, and the recently liberated colonials now attribute to the imperialist Western Allies, the unrelenting extraction of reparations and retributions from the collectively accused will still not correct injustice, but merely reverse the roles. It turns the previous villains into complying serfs now humbly labouring for their redemption, and the previous victims into imperious villains enjoying the power of the whip. It transforms the meek into bullies while reducing the former bullies to guilt-stricken do-gooders accepting their current humiliation with masochistic glee. It substitutes the massacres of Stanleyville for the massacres of Amritsar, until the appetite for compensation is stilled, and the scales begin once again to tip to the other side cancelling out all gains. For the consequences of satiation are always the same. The victor softens while the defeated emerges cleansed and steeled but also outraged by the hardship of a punishment inflicted a generation too long, with the result that the close of the cycle may find the compensation-drugged victor down, and the defeated on top of him once more.

This is why, by suppressing the uninvolved successors of the Kaiser after the first world war, the West did not get peace but Hitler and a second world war—all in stubborn pursuit of an emotionally understandable and highly gratifying but rationally untenable and hence historically self-defeating collective-guilt principle. And the same thing happened after the second world war, when the compensatory dismantlement of the industrial equipment of Germany resulted not in the weakening but in the strengthening of her economy. It left the victors with her obsolete machinery while providing the punished enemy with the chance of replacing it with the latest in efficiency and design by which it subsequently outcompeted the victors.

Thus, even if there *were* moral justifications behind the madness, a philosophy of compensation would still be madness, and would confront the leaders of the underdeveloped countries with the same kind of rude awakening, if they indulge in it too long, that ended the feverish retribution dream of the Western Allies. Instead of achieving a comfortably secure freedom—a self-contradictory target considering that freedom is an aspect not of comfort but of hardship overcome in daily struggle—they may suddenly find themselves immersed in a second age of colonialism with an exasperated Russia and America, tired of being perpetually pitted against each other, making common cause against all those now thriving on their conflict.

And lastly, I can not share the assumption that the underdeveloped nations should have a moral claim on "the then poor but now rich developed countries" on the ground that the latter have amassed their riches at the expense of the retardation of the present colonial or newly liberated peoples through the "forced contributions made by generations of their sweated and bullied ancestors." They have amassed their riches by sweating and bullying, all right. But, as Marx, apostle of the exploited, has so forcefully tried to prove, the primary victims of their sweating and bullying were the ancestors of their own rather than of their colonial labour force. Having them so much nearer to exploit, the establishment of these countries did not begin colonization in order to get rich. They began it in order to secure foreign markets for the overspill of their already *existing* riches extracted from surplus value withheld from their *domestic* labour, and piling up *after* domestic capital accumulation had reached such proportions that its fruit could no longer be absorbed on the home market by the sweated, bullied, and underpaid workers producing it.

Colonization and imperial expansion were thus generally the consequence rather than the cause of domestic riches. There were some exceptions as in the case of the Roman empire, when advanced countries were themselves colonized by invading colonials. But otherwise the sequence was always the same. Wealth caused colonization, not colonization wealth, if for no other reason than that only the wealthy could afford the cost of colonial conquest. Which does of course not mean that colonization, like any investment, did not produce secondary margins of *added* wealth for the expanding establishment and the growing business community in both colonies and motherland. But it never bene-fitted the workers whose living standards remained as depressed in the motherland as in the colonies. Actually, the "forced con-tributions" extracted from the workers of the motherland were even more onerous considering that, being more efficiently em-ployed, the surplus value withheld from them was by nature much larger than what could have been withheld from the infinitely less efficiently employed colonial labour force. This holds even if one takes into account the generally lower position of colonial subsistence levels. But if one can barely keep one's head above the water, it makes little difference whether the water level is at high or low altitude. One nearly drowns in either.

10. *Empire of Destitution*

Now it is true that most of what I have just said is contradic-ted by an impressive array of witnesses cited by Professor Thorne. They range from Adam Smith, Clapham, Cunningham, Ashton, Ashworth, all the way up to that most famous of all imperialists, Winston Churchill. Yet, with all my admiration for them, I feel that, in this particular instance, their strength is not their author-ity, but, as Anatol Murad would say, the *unanimity* of their error. This applies particularly also to the slightly "jingoistic" figures produced by Winston Churchill, who thought in 1928 that Eng-land's annual income of close to $1.5 billion from territorial investments explained the source from which Great Britain was "able to defray social services at a level incomparably higher than that of any European country, or any country."

However, I am reminded of another occasion, when the same Winston Churchill denied during a hearing in London the funds requested by Professor Thorne's distinguished father for an extended educational programme in the then colony of British Guiana on the ground that, according to another set of figures, they simply could not be mobilized. Mr. Thorne's reply, at the time, was that, having been interested in Mr. Churchill's career from his early school days, he was not convinced that interpreta-tion of figures was one of his strong points. I do not recall Mr.

Churchill's answer to this elegant counter-thrust. But it did induce the chivalrous British leader at the end of the meeting to extend his hand and, congratulating Mr. Thorne on the way in which he defended his cause by attack, to come forth with a characteristically Churchillian appreciation of a battle gallantly fought: "Mr. Thorne, I admire people who know how to fire back."

Well, I am not more impressed by Winston Churchill's figures than was Professor Thorne's illustrious father. In fact, enrolling at the London School of Economics as an impressionable student from an impoverished Austria the very year Mr. Churchill praised British social service "jingoistically" as the highest in the world, I remember vividly my dismay at discovering how poorly they compared with those of recently defeated and empire-less Austria or Germany, whose social services were then considered models of achievement.

So what Mr. Churchill's figures mean to me, and must have meant to the masses of British labour, is that, in spite of an annual income from territorial investments to the amount of $1.5 billion, so little could be spared for improving British social services that, tired of the rising misery in the midst of imperial bombast, a less jingoistic electorate installed the second Labour Government in English history soon afterwards. This should not suggest that I doubt Mr. Churchill's figures. I doubt their significance as to the cause of British prosperity. Belgians also extracted vast sums from their territorial investments in the Congo. Yet, presented in their proper context, they amounted to a measly 1% to 2% of the country's national income,[1] indicating how little colonial exploitation contributed to the *social* wealth of developed nations.

However, this still leaves me with the evidence and figures cited by Professor Thorne from greater economic authorities than Winston Churchill. Also in their case I have no reason to dispute their validity. For colonial enterprises, like domestic enterprises did of course produce new wealth for both established and new entrepreneurs. Moreover, they were undoubtedly also

[1] See Austin Robinson. *The Economic Consequences of the Size of Nations.* London: Macmillan, 1960. p. 357.

amongst the most profitable business ventures. But aside from their effect of creating or increasing the wealth of a number of individuals, I can see little evidence suggesting that, unlike Belgium's meagre 1% to 2% increment, they added more than a mere drop to the bucket of domestic net national income in the case of Great Britain. In fact, seen in the context of their *social* impact, the benefit of their riches seems to have been nil, if one considers what I believe is an infinitely more revealing set of figures. These are the statistics collected over the span of half a century by Joseph Rowntree who, unlike the authorities cited by Professor Thorne, viewed the riches of empire not from the perspective of the members of the imperial establishment but from the perspective of the members of the imperial working class.

According to Rowntree, 27.84% of the citizens of his native York (30.7% in the case of London), or 43% if one speaks only in terms of the working class, were found to be in a state of destitution in 1899—when the power and glory of the British empire was its pinnacle. According to the same author, this figure still stood at a shocking 31% in 1936, seven years after Mr. Churchill's speech, when the empire was no longer quite so impressive, but still in command of the tremendous area of India. Only by 1951, when the empire was at last all but liquidated, did the figure of working class destitution show a dramatic change, shrivelling in the space of a few years to a mere 3%—a residuum due to old age, no longer to low wages.

Thus, as I have elaborated in greater detail elsewhere,[1] whatever the connection between the two developments, and in spite of the almost unanimous professional opinion to the contrary, the fact stands out that, the greater the empire of Britain overseas, the worse the destitution she suffered at home. By contrast, the more she lost in colonies overseas, the higher became her living standard at home. The more she shrank in expanse, the easier it was to divert her resources from the power to the welfare state, and turn destitution into affluence. As John Strachey has pointed out in one of his last publications, *The Great Awakening*,[2] the profit possibilities of the welfare-centred domestic market were at last discovered to be so much greater than those resting on

[1] *Cambridge Opinion*, November 1962.
[2] London: Encounter, 1961 (pamphlet series).

the diseconomies of overexpanded overseas possessions that Britain's former colonies are suffering from a reflex reaction to a stimulus long past, if they fear a return to imperialism on the part of a former master who, by his own admission, has never had it so good, now that he has been relieved of their administration.

Answering a letter, in which I had asked for confirmation that I was not misinterpreting his conclusions, John Strachey reasserted his as well as my idea of the social unprofitability of imperial exploitation though he disagreed with my interpretation that Britain's recent rise to general affluence was due to her loss of empire and consequent reduction in size. As a socialist, he preferred to attribute it to the establishment of the welfare state. My reply was to the effect that, while the wide spread of current British affluence was indeed the result of the new distributive system introduced by the welfare state; the welfare state itself was the result of the loss of empire. For no country, be it capitalist or socialist, could have borne the high cost of imperial domination and the high cost of a welfare state, with all this entails in expanded social services, at the same time. It had to choose either the one or the other, considering that the vastness of empire— "bright and brittle," as St. Augustine says in *The City of God* (IV, 3), "and evermore in fear and danger of breaking"—cannot be administered without withholding from the mass of workers a large share of what could otherwise be distributed among them. But if such a large share must be withheld for covering the cost of empire, it goes without saying that the welfare state, based as it is on higher wages, is an unattainable target during the former's lifetime. Which explains why the socialist parties of imperialist states are forever driven to link their claim for economic improvement with the simultaneous demand for the dismantlement of empire. They could obviously never sell their people on the latter if empire were indeed the source rather than the voracious devourer of riches.

What the statesmen of former colonies seem therefore consistently to overlook, when they consider it not undignified to demand from Harold Wilson compensation for what was done by Benjamin Disraeli, is that empires—the imperial state, that is— can flourish only in one way: by keeping not only the colonial but also the metropolitan labour masses at the lowest possible standard of living. And what Marxists consistently overlook is that not only capitalist but also socialist capital accumulation; and not only capital accumulation but also the excessive needs of any large-scale territorial administration, be it of an empire such as Great Britain's, or of China, the Soviet Union, the Congo, Brazil, necessitates the living-standard=depressing withholding of surplus value from the only victim that can reliably yield it in the enormous quantities that are required—the mass of working men.[1]

11. Non-Imperial Sources of Wealth

It is because of this that I have questioned not only the economic horse-sense but also the moral justification of the assistance claims of underdeveloped societies. It might be different if at least the imperial *state,* if not the imperial *people,* owed its wealth to pilfering the colonies. But not even this can be maintained. It owed everything but its frills to itself.

It owed its first increment in wealth, *agricultural capital,* to the surpluses gained in the medieval dimness of its pre-imperial village-state phase by putting its own (not other people's) labour to more efficient use on land. It achieved its *second* increment during its still pre-imperial city-state phase by beginning to withhold surplus value again from its own (not other people's) labour, and diverting the thus arising first wave of *non*-agricultural surpluses from consumption to the creation of *manufacturing capital*. It produced its *third* increment by putting the second to work, thereby creating a new variety of *non*-agricultural surpluses which took the form of *industrial* and *commercial capital*.

However, since the available distribution system had as yet no social mechanism for allocating the constantly increasing sur-

[1] This is why Marx's appeal to the workers of the world to unite must necessarily be self-defeating. Their unity would create such a colossal social structure embracing them that, again, so much surplus value would have to be withheld from their wages to support it that, as George Orwell has so brilliantly envisioned, even a socialist distribution system could achieve nothing but a subsistence-level existence, and constant supervision on top of it. A worker-unifying organization would be like a 400-floor skyscraper, which would need so many elevators for servicing that not a square inch could be left for using the structure for anything but the running of elevators.

pluses to the improvement of the consumption standards of the workers helping to produce them, the *fourth* increment to social wealth that now began to bubble up assumed the shape of *immaterial or urban capital.* This no longer added so much to the stock of wealth as to the beauty of its form and the wholesomeness of its communal arrangement, the fruit of which—fountains, loggias, galleries, architecture, taste, and a new style rather than a new level of living—for once also the workers could consume. But not even at this culminating stage did imperialist exploitation have anything to do with the increase in social riches. On the contrary! What caused this latest accumulation was the very opposite: not the existence but the absence of far-flung imperial involvement; not huge colonial markets but the low cost of the continued small size of the economically now fully matured political community. Thus also urban capital accrued as a result of local, not other people's, talent and labour.

However, with this a turning point was reached. Still unable to come forth with a new distributive system under the spreading shadow of Calvin's life-negating double principle that encouraged both high production and low consumption at the same time, some of the now no longer at all poor societies started to burst at their seams. As a result, to relieve themselves of the pressure of continuously accumulating surpluses—which in earlier periods were more sensibly spent on debauching the populace[1]—they created new outlets for them by transforming them this time into *military capital* or, as one might call it in contrast to urban capital, *national and imperial capital.* Instead of having to commit a mounting number of workers released from an increasingly efficient production process as beggars to the street, this made it possible to reabsorb them in new industries of scale and particularly in the henceforth indispensable receptacle of technological unemployment: the standing armies, which could always be put to use

---

[1] An idea of pre-imperial wealth can be obtained from the following censorious account of Pasquale Villari in his *Life and Times of Savonarola* (New York: Charles Scribner, 1896, p. 45) on Lorenzo il Magnifico who "encouraged all the worst tendencies of the age and multiplied its corruption. Abandoned to pleasure himself, he urged the people to lower depth of abandonment in order to plunge them into the lethargy of intoxication. In fact, during his reign Florence was a continuous scene of revelry and dissipation." Which colony ever provided this for its imperial homeland? None.

by a culminated city-state when it set out on the aggressive and hyperactive road of first nation and then empire building. Hence, even imperial capital was created by exploiting originally local, not colonial, labour.

However, what an expansion-bent society soon discovered was that, instead of opening up a fifth source of net riches, both empires and large-nation states cost as much as they brought in. They effectively used up the overspill of Calvinist surpluses, but at the same time deprived those who indulged in the cancerous luxury of functionless overgrowth of the chance of any further social advance until the rage was spent. True, they produced the *immaterial* increment of glory and grandeur which, like urban beauty, could be consumed by the entire society that created it but, unlike urban beauty, was an opiate that drugged rather than enhanced the existence of the citizen. And as to the *material* substance they generated, this took the form of *remedial* commodities which, instead of adding to living standards at home, merely produced the means for coping less efficiently with the greater hardships of life on an irrationally extended scale.

This is why imperial capital cities could rarely add more to the pre-imperial splendour of their core than ever widening circles of slums; or why none of them, with all the remedial riches extracted from their colonies for the building of railroads and other costly integration commodities, ever managed to surpass in architectural glory and truly social wealth such centres of small states as Siena, Lucca, Salzburg, Dresden, Prague, Troyes, which never knew empire and, indeed, were completed and prosperous long before modern nation-states were born. On the other hand, the one empire that seems never to have passed through the dissipation-preventing and wealth-begetting phase of uninvolved city-state development, Ethiopia, is to this day more retarded than even the former colonies surrounding it.

Thus, far from having generated the wealth of the "then poor and now rich developed countries," imperial expansion actually arrested their further *domestic* development. It cancelled out any chance for a real increment in wealth other than the neurotic satisfaction of national glory and imperial grandeur by consuming all it produced either in imperial administration or in the indispensable accumulation of *colonial* capital which, as a result of its location in the exploited areas, benefitted in the end paradoxically, though not intentionally, the subsequent liberated colonial state more than the receding imperial one.[1]

Only *after* the empires had been dismantled, and *after* their heartlands had been freed of the burden of excessive size by contracting once again to their more manageable earlier confines, did it become possible for them to resume their long interrupted road towards their own further development. As the strange set of Rowntree statistics demonstrate, not only could they now proceed with the addition of a *fifth net* increment to their national wealth in the form of *welfare capital;* the introduction at last of

---

[1] To judge by the "unbullied" retardation of Ethiopia, colonies might never have developed this capital on their own, had they been spared the bitter passage through empire, bitter more in retrospect than in the course of the passage. In fact, many, though not all, colonies were in a material sense actually the only lasting beneficiaries of imperialism—which I trust will not be taken as a sign of imperialism on my part. Myrdal (*op. cit.*, p. 56, 57) makes the same point when he writes "the economic activities of the colonizers represented a measure of spread of economic expansion which without the peculiar power relations of colonialism would not have taken place. Thailand, which thanks to jealousies between colonial powers was left in political independence, did not become more developed than Burma. . . . During the time of dependence . . . the colonies probably had more development than if they had been left to themselves."

While I was quoting the Rowntree figures, according to which the British rate of destitution had, since the establishment of the welfare state, declined to a mere 3%, which, moreover, was no longer due to low wages but to old age, my wife received the following touching letter from one of the remaining 3%, her uncomplaining former maid from England, making one wonder why with all its past colonial exploitation a now rich succession state to empire should still be so poor as to be unable to help the most pitiful segment of destitute, the old: "Well my dear," she writes, "your kind friend from the Slad took us to see Mrs. Musty the Tuesday before Christmas she was quite all right only she kept on about wanting some money, I was down to my last 5 bob. Maud and Mrs. Meadows could not afford to give her any. As we did take almost everything we could think of. Poor old Annie Price passed away on Dec. 8th in her sleep. Eunice seems to have gone right back ever since and she may have to go into hospital herself. Mrs. Millard is now much better. I feel much better myself, only my left foot is so very painful.—Mr. Merryweather told me my general health will not stand another opp so they are having some shoes made for me. They do not come under the N.H. [National Health] so I've to save all my spare money for when they are ready.—Mrs. King is fine she's been here for a week, Mrs. Carpenter sends

a new distributive system by post-imperial socialist governments could for the first time release part of the surplus value—which previously had to be withheld to secure the overextended complex of empire in the face of the colossal dangers besetting it from without and within—to the workers who had created it.

But only *part* of it. For even the welfare state of the former imperial powers must still withhold disproportionately large amounts for the purpose of administering home territories which, in spite of their reduced dimensions, are today exposed to very much greater and hence costlier pressures of scale than they were during their pre-imperial phase, when their populations were of lesser effective size both because of their smaller numbers and the considerably looser degree of integration.

If therefore a more significant share of surplus value is to be returned to the workers, the penitent former imperial powers will gain nothing either by restoring imperial dimensions in the form of common markets, or by improving the post-capitalist welfare state by means of still more socialism and still higher productivity. What they must do is go beyond mere imperial contraction and reduce, for good measure, the size also of their metropolitan societies in one of two ways: outright dismemberment, or federal devolution into a meshwork of highly self-sufficient political entities of such small size that the cost of their corporate upkeep will no longer be of the guns-or-butter variety. Then, and only then, can social survival be ensured without the need of pauperizing the citizen in 1984 fashion.

In other words, the condition capable of creating the long-delayed *sixth* increment of social wealth is no longer, as in the

her very grateful thanks to you; she may come here for an afternoon visit tomorrow. Sorry to say there is no improvement in Diane. She gave up another job her mother 'as not received one penny from her two months, she's a very big girl to keep about.—Well, Dear, write again when you have time, Love N." Is this the riches of empire? It makes one appreciate St. Augustine's question in his *City of God* (III, 10): "Why should any empire make disquiet the scale unto greatness? In this little world of man's body, is it not better to have a mean stature with an unmoved health than a huge bigness with intolerable sickness? To take no rest at the point when thou shouldst rest, the end, but still to confound the greater growth with the greater grief?"

case of the other five, improved technology, exploitation of labour, welfare state, or new socialist distributive systems. It is the small size of a matured political community. In contrast to welfare capital, this sixth and climactic increment may be called *luxury capital,* an accumulation made possible by low cost rather than high investment, and distinguished by two characteristics:

1. Its yield is able to improve not only the social but also the personal standard of living. It adds to the quality of life not so much by bettering the structure *of* the subsistence level as by raising the individual *above* it. It provides him not with a more efficient swimming equipment for keeping him afloat at a higher water level, but with the chance of climbing at last out of the water altogether on to the relaxing shore where he does not need an improved swimming equipment because he no longer needs to swim. And 2, unlike welfare capital, luxury capital can be materially distributed among the workers not because of a more equitable sharing system, which is meaningless in communities so large and complex that nothing can be spared for sharing; it can be distributed because it is no longer needed to cope with the insignificant problems of societies of moderate size which are yet large enough in Aristotle's terms to furnish the implements of the good life not so much to the community as to all its individual members.

Thus, with the exception of colonial capital, practically all the sources of social wealth in the "once poor and now rich developed countries" have been the result of a combination of two factors dating back to pre-imperial times: the rising productivity of *local* labour power, and the continued *small* dimensions of a matured political community. It was this that accounted for their rise, as the glamorous Renaissance city-states have so amply demonstrated, not imperial exploitation which yielded the neurotic income of grandeur to the afflicted, but otherwise was a hopeless loss proposition except, paradoxically, as Gunnar Myrdal implied, for the exploited colonies—which, I trust, will not make me suspect as an apologist of colonialism. All I meant to convey is Horace's exhortation in *Carmina* (II, 3, 1): *Omitte mirari beatae fumum et opes strepitumque Romae*—stop admiring the smoke, wealth, and noise of prosperous Rome.

Author's Reply

12. The Dragging Effect of National Size

Whatever one may say of my sequence of development stages, at which I have arrived not by ignoring but by reading history, in one thing I remain particularly unshaken. Both Professor Thorne and I agree that the imperial stage has retarded and exploited the colonies (which does not mean that, as Ethopia has shown, they might not have remained even more retarded and exploited without passing through that phase). But in spite of the unanimity of opinion ranging from Adam Smith to Winston Churchill and Alfred Thorne, I still maintain, without being a Marxist myself, with Marx, Strachey, and Rowntree that empires left the exploiting imperial peoples just as destitute as the colonials,[1] and that, just as the colonies required economic liberation, so the imperial peoples required redistribution through nationalization, to get access to a greater share in the wealth surrounding them.

Moreover, with neither Smith nor Marx to lean upon in this instance, I remain specially unshaken in my central conviction. This is that the real dragging effect of empire had its primary cause neither in imperial nor in capitalist exploitation. As also such giant socialist and "non-imperial" countries as the Soviet Union or China are belatedly discovering, the primary cause lay in the excessive territorial *size* that empire implies. Just as excessive weight is inherently oppressive without regard to its intent, so excessive political size, weighed down by the gigantic proportions of the state apparatus it requires to maintain itself, constitutes inherently such a mass that all life is stifled that tries to develop underneath it.

This is why, seemingly unlike most of my contemporaries, I can see no difference between imperialists clinging to huge territories and socialists or "nationalists" doing the same thing. It makes no difference whether the country in question is Russia, China, the Congo, Nigeria, Ghana, Brazil, Pakistan, or India. The

[1] One might add as witness another eminent Marxist, George Lichtheim who, following closely E. J. Hobsbawm's earlier argument in *Industry and Empire,* notes in his *Imperialism* (London: Allen Lane, 1971) how the vast export of British capital that went with imperial expansion actually retarded industrial growth at home, in spite of the profit it brought to individual developers.

167

millstone around their neck is not their imperial heritage but the senseless hugeness of their holdings. And as long as these are not broken up by their megalomaniacal leaders into manageable "development principalities," they will stay retarded in freedom as much as in subjection, and fleece their citizens of the fruit of their labour under socialist direction as much as under free enterprise, under men such as Chiang Kai-shek as much as under Castro, with loans as much as without them, with world markets as much as in isolation, and, I am afraid, under Alfred Thorne as much as under Leopold Kohr.

13. *Misuse of Aid by Reactionaries*

This is, finally, also why I cannot go along with Professor Thorne's suggestion that the reason for the failure of aid, extended particularly to Latin American countries, is its use not for economic development, for which it is earmarked, but for the military purpose of protecting reactionary governments from communism. I am quite sure this is correct, and I have also in this instance no doubt whatever in the reliability of my friend's evidence, drawn both from direct sources of information and wide personal experience.

But I see nothing unusual in this, as I have myself maintained that all aid corrupts and, if united with absolute power, corrupts absolutely or, as someone suggested: deliciously. Nor, however, am I able to see any difference between "reactionary" governments abusing aid for protecting themselves from communism, and "progressive" governments abusing it for building up huge armies as in Cuba, North Vietnam, or North Korea, in order to protect themselves from reaction. Both are at this juncture using the symbols of economic grandeur such as steel mills or cement factories not so much for housing and other social improvements as for missiles, guns, and related incidentals of war, as are regularly paraded on national auditing day. These parades are, moreover, physically so impressive that I am sure Professor Thorne will spare me the effort to list the comparative figures indicating the amounts of resources allocated by "progressive" governments on the one hand to military purposes to keep the bosses in power, and on the other to development purposes that might benefit the civilian needs of the people. If even rich Italy under Mussolini had to make her people choose between guns, to calm their emotional longings, and butter, to satisfy their material needs, I cannot see how *doctores* Castro, Obote, or Nkrumah, with their much poorer resources could have offered both at the same time— unless, of course, like their reactionary Latin American colleagues, they too were surreptitiously financing their self-protective military establishment by abusing foreign aid—as it turned out in the case of at least the two latter: to no avail.

Actually, what threatens the existence of both "reactionary" and "progressive" types of government is for each not the other, but the mounting evidence of ineptitude on the part of either in coping with the problems of scale arising from the disproportionately large size of their current domains. The oversize that led to the demise of empire, is bound to lead also to their own undoing, as giant Pakistan and Nigeria are already experiencing. So what both types of government are really trying to do is to protect themselves from being overthrown not so much by their rivals as by their own peoples, on whom it might suddenly dawn that their scale-enlarged problems are so far beyond the measure of their leaders, or any leader, that neither type can ever be expected to ensure them a better life.

And it is this, the impotence of the leaders of underdeveloped countries (as of any other country) to cope with the problems of excessive size—not reaction—that forces all of them, not just the reactionaries, to divert an inordinate chunk of aid into the hands of the military. For the best way of keeping the mass of people both in check and reconciled with its deprivation has always been the patriotically proclaimed need for Spartan military preparedness against a sinister adversary. Indeed so essential is such an adversary—the reactionary to the progressive; the communist to the reactionary—for covering up the abysmal failure of leaders to deliver the good life in countries which are too big that, paraphrasing Voltaire, one may say that, if an adversary did not exist, in the interest of governmental survival it would be necessary to create him.

The only way to prevent the military use of economic aid is thus not by replacing a reactionary government with a progressive one. It is by making the fund-consuming, defence-requiring, failure-hiding reactionary or progressive, real or imaginary adversary dispensable by giving the governments in power the chance of proving themselves in things other than the art of teaching their soldiers how to die with patriotic fervour and the name of their boss on their lips. But the chance for positive social achievement—taking the form, for example, not of deceptively *raising* the subsistence level, but of insuring to the workers a life *above* the subsistence level—cannot materialize unless the size of the political unit under the sway of any single leader is brought down to fit the measure of man. The good society is not one that requires a costly genius, but one uninvolved enough to be able to do without one. This alone is crisis-proof.

Thus, as for a time Cato ended all his speeches by demanding that Carthage be destroyed, so my *ceterum censeo* is once again that all big-area states, these "monsters of mercantilism" as Henry Simons has called them in his *Economic Policy for a Free Society,*[1] must be dismantled if anything but the inhuman self-interest of the state is to be served. In *The Breakdown of Nations* I advocated this with regard to the *Big Powers,* a proposition with which, I am sure, the underdeveloped countries will wholeheartedly agree. Here I extend it to underdeveloped countries. Unless their size is reduced, the only alternative ultimately open to them will be the same as for every filled-up integrated large-area state: total militarization. This will provide them with something to parade with. But it will deprive their citizens in the name of progress of what earlier generations have withheld from them in the name of kings, or gods, or eternal life, all opiates for the masses, under whatever name they may go. *Plus ça change, plus il reste la même chose.*

14. *Summation, Constantine, and Ricardo*

Summing up: I feel that, where Professor Thorne and I differ, is not so much in the facts from which we evolve our systems, as in the systems we evolve from our facts. None of the data and quotations he assembled in his fruitful and welcome criticism do I challenge. His ammunition is excellent. In fact I hope to use

[1] Chicago University Press, 1948, p. 125.

much of it myself. Where we differ is the direction in which we
fire it off.

We agree that underdeveloped countries have been retarded,
exploited, and stunted in their economic growth by the empires
of which they formed part. We do not agree on who was the bene-
ficiary of this exploitation. Professor Thorne seems to think it
was the imperialist *society* of the *motherland*. I feel it was the
capitalist *establishment* of the *empire,* which includes the colonial
elite. We agree that exploitation meant victims. We do not agree
on the identity of the victims. Professor Thorne seems to think
they were the exploited colonies. I feel they were the exploited
masses of workers in both colonies and motherland. Destitution
is not any sweeter in the fogs of London than in the palm groves
of Loiza Aldea. We agree on the need for development. We do
not agree, it seems, whether development should follow the historic way, tackling subsequent phases only when prior phases
are completed, or the hodgepodge way, building irrigation canals
and Hilton Hotels at the same time. Nor do we agree whether it
should be financed by foreign borrowing or domestic saving;
whether it should be achieved by softening the rigors of life or,
like Avis, by trying harder; by producing for the massive needs
of a world market or for the infinite variety of domestic demand;
by improving the terms of trade through an increase in trade or a
reduction in trade; by orating before the United Nations or by
preparing greatness in privacy and secrecy, "far away from all
distraction"; with aid or without aid.

And lastly, while agreeing on a number of secondary causes
explaining the nature and predicament of underdevelopment, we
do not seem to agree on the primary cause. This refers not to the
agent presiding over the process of retardation, nor to the *beni-
ficiary* which may have been empire or capitalism, but might also
have been socialism, had it existed on an imperial scale as it now
does in China and the Soviet Union; it refers to the material *circumstance* that was bound to produce retardation even if the
leaders had been apostles of advance.

Since the question of primary cause, though colouring everything I have written during the past 20 years, did not arise in this
discussion, I do not presume to sum up Professor Thorne's answer

in this respect beyond suggesting that he probably thinks otherwise. But I can restate my own position. This is that the primary cause retarding regions even if all other conditions for rapid advance are given—human, social, political, technological, economic—is not empire, or capitalism, but *territorial size* of such dimensions that bungling, fumbling, distortion, inefficiency, wastes, exploitation result because man's small stature simply cannot cope with them. That is why in the last analysis the imperial homelands could themselves resume the road towards progress only *after* the loss of their vast holdings.

But the cancer of excessive size has not only distorted the homelands. It still affects the territorial immensity of the now liberated former colonies created in simplicist sweep over vast stretches of continents that looked like Irish counties from the perspective of the remote billiard tables of London, on which many of them were designed. And it is this, as I see it, that is the main obstacle to their current advance: not the divine cunning of neo-imperialists, but the megalomaniacal appetites for power, land, and human masses of their own leaders trying to preserve the primary cause responsible for the retardation of their peoples—excessive size; proportions beyond the scope of the human mind.

And this being the case, as seen from the perspective and experience of my own small stature, I remain convinced—in spite of the valuable things I have learned from my debate with my cherished and much admired friend—that the first step towards development, with help as much as without it, lies in the dissolution of all excessively large political entities into humanly manageable small *CUV* communities. Then there will be infinite chances for Peisistratean leaders and Periclean reapers of fruits to discharge a historic mission. Otherwise our time will merely duplicate tre sterile age of the Caesars with all their pomp, ceremony, executions, deifications, oratory, publicity, giving us an existence full of filmed and recorded sound and fury, signifying nothing.

And with this I rest my case. Emulating "the example of the Greek philosophers, who could maintain their arguments without losing their temper, and assert their freedom without violating their friendship,"[1] I am shaken neither in my friendship nor in my argument by the well documented criticism of Professor Thorne. Rather I feel like David Ricardo who, when concluding a long debate with a famous friend, wrote: "And now my dear Malthus I have done. Like other disputants after much discussions we each retain our own opinion. These discussions however never influence our friendship; I should not like you more than I do if you agreed in opinion with me."[1] Which goes for me too!

[1] Constantine's recommendation to the clergy of Alexandria which evidently did *not* follow the example of the Greek philosophers. Gibbon. *Decline and Fall of the Roman Empire.* Philadelphia: Henry T. Coates, no date, Vol. II, p. 228.

[1] *Ricardo's Development as an Economist,* by Joseph M. Gillman. *Science & Society,* Vol. XX, No. 3 (Summer 1956), p. 225.

"You ain't gaining much altitude
holding me down."

MAULDIN

Chapter Three

COMMENTS BY
PROFESSOR ROBERT J. ALEXANDER

*Speaking of getting help from outside reminds
one of using as much as possible what we have
at home as the basis of nation-building.*
—Dr. Kenneth Kaunda

As is always the case with the writings of Professor Kohr, *Development Without Aid* is stimulating and thought provoking. It has a big enough germ of truth to be challenging, but as is true with most protagonists of new and different ideas, Professor Kohr claims much too much for his model of economic development.

Professor Kohr writes as if this was a world in which, aside from a handful of highly industrialized nations, all other countries were completely underdeveloped. Perhaps if he had written his book in 1900 his picture of the world would, in this regard, have been closer to the truth. The fact is that at the present time there are few truly underdeveloped countries.

Thus, it makes no sense to tell the Brazilians, whose country as a whole is still underdeveloped, but who have in Sao Paulo and its vicinity one of the world's most highly developed industrial centres, to go back to the age of handicrafts and start all over again, as does Professor Kohr. It doesn't even make much sense to tell this to the Costa Ricans, who already have a cement, textile, shoe and leather industry, and a well developed hydroelectric system. Perhaps Professor Kohr's formula would be applicable to Sikkim and Bhutan or to West Irian but I cannot think of many other parts of the world where lack of modern development is so total as to make his model applicable.

Another fundamental aspect of the presently underdeveloped countries which Professor Kohr ignores is the fact that they are all more or less closely tied in with the world market. Even a

Comments by Professor Robert J. Alexander

very poor country like Bolivia is integrated into world trade. Certainly, such more advanced nations as Ceylon, Ghana, or the Ivory Coast are very much in the world market.

Again, in this connection, the underdeveloped countries of today—which are really "underdeveloped" and not undeveloped—are not starting from scratch. A large segment of their communities—and usually the most powerful element—gets its income and power from this connection with the world market. An increasingly large part of the population gets its living by providing services or goods for an impersonal market. To suddenly destroy this connection as would be necessary if Professor Kohr's model were to be followed, would mean in the case of Argentina, or Cuba, or Chile, or Lebanon, or Syria, or Israel, the complete dislocation of the great majority of the population and their return to a status which they had long since surpassed. In other countries, such as Mexico, Brazil, Chile, or Egypt, it would mean the complete disruption of the lives of pretty close to a majority of the population. In addition, it should be noted that those who live outside the market are for the most part exactly elements of the population who have little interest in development in any case.

All of this leads one to reject Professor Kohr's hypothesis that because the first industrial countries, those of Western Europe, developed towards industrialism more or less in the way he sketches in his model, there is something "natural" about that particular method of development. Certainly other countries which are today in the "developed" category, came to industrialization in quite a different manner.

The United States, for instance, did not develop according to the West European pattern. The United States has never been a country of purely local markets, such as was medieval Europe, and such as are the towns of Professor Kohr's model. From the beginning, the 13 original colonies were deeply involved in world trade—providing tobacco, anil, sugar, fish, ships' stores, slaves to Europe and to other parts of America. Only on the outer reaches of the frontier was the farmer truly a subsistence farmer, and then only for a few short years until the general population caught up with him. Thus there never existed the process of isolated towns growing together, first to trade with one another and then to trade a bit with the outside world, which Professor Kohr describes. Towns grew up because they were apt centres to handle the commerce with the outside world, which was from the beginning the focus of attention of the surrounding agricultural hinterland.

During the period of the United States' most rapid development, it grew in a manner diametrically opposed to the Kohr model. It turned out massive exports of agricultural products which were sold to Europe in return for the capital equipment which was needed by the U.S. Furthermore, there was a large flow of foreign private investment (the "foreign aid" of the period) to build the railroads, and a range of industries. It would appear to me that this was just as "natural" a way for a country to achieve a state of high economic development as was the pattern followed by Western Europe three of four centuries earlier. It is much closer to the path actually being trod by most presently developing countries.

The fact is that Europe in the period between 1300 and 1750 had no alternative but to develop along the lines that it did. There were then no "developed" countries, in the sense of highly industrialized ones, all of the European nations were more or less on the same level. There *are* alternative methods of development in the 20th Century, and the mere fact that the first industrial countries developed along Dr. Kohr's pattern does not make that pattern sacrosanct. In plotting a course for the presently developing countries, one should not ignore what has happened since the beginning of the Industrial Revolution in Europe two centuries ago.

It seems to me somehow absurd that in a world which is not that of Europe of the 14th to 18th Century, but rather that of the 20th Century, the presently developing nations should be required —as Professor Kohr wishes to require of them—to go through four centuries themselves before they can be highly developed; why they should have to go through all of the phases which Western Europe experienced, ignoring completely the fact that there now *do* exist highly industrialized nations. This is not only absurd but impossible. The developing nations are quite aware of the existence of the industrialized countries, and they put a premium on speed in their own development. This emphasis is underscored, incidentally, by a factor completely ignored by Professor Kohr, the population explosion, which means that in Brazil, for instance, it is necessary to find 1,000,000 new jobs each year.

Furthermore, the analogy which Professor Kohr draws between the process of development which he outlines—essentially that of Europe between 1300 and 1750, it must again be emphasized—is fallacious. This Western European process of development is not the inevitable process of an individual who is growing to maturity. An equally apt analogy might be the training of a soldier. The modern military establishment does not find it necessary to first train a soldier with a club, then with a slingshot, then with a bow and arrow, then with a cross-bow, then with a harquebus, then with a breech loading rifle, then with an automatic weapon of the most modern model. Rather, it trains the modern soldier with the modern weapon. Just so, the country which wants to develop in the 20th Century does so with the facilities available in the 20th Century, not with those which were available in the 13th.

One of these modern facilities is assistance from the already industrialized nations. This assistance is not necessarily charity. Admittedly charity is not healthy as a long-run proposition either on a personal level or a national one, a point which Dr. Kohr makes abundantly clear. But "foreign aid", whether it be in the form of private investment or intergovernmental loans or grants, should be and usually is a matter of enlightened self-interest on the part of the industrialized countries involved. The fact is that the underdeveloped countries for the most part are not good trading partners—except when they are themselves developing. Most of the world's trade is between the highly developed nations. It is therefore in the long-run interest of the already developed countries to help in one way or another the development of those which have so far lagged behind.

Furthermore, history indicates that foreign assistance has been of very great aid in the furthering of the development of the more backward nations. We have already indicated the case of the United States in the 19th Century, which profited considerably from foreign investment. In most presently developing countries, the first major impetus for modernization and development came from foreign investment, which established railroads, public utilities, modern banking enterprises, key manufacturing plants and so on. This was certainly not done out of a feeling of charity, and the foreign firms generally did quite well from their activities —but the fact remains that these activities were of key importance, both in arousing the desire for further development, and in establishing the first infrastructure on which such development could be based.

Of course, one is tempted to feel that Professor Kohr thinks that many of the aspects of modern economic development should not exist in any case—modern means of transport, perhaps large-scale modern industry, many of the consumers' gadgets of the highly developed countries. These are usually exactly the things for which it is necessary to obtain foreign exchange, and in the obtaining of which, therefore, foreign assistance of some kind looms large. If this is the message which he is trying to get across, it is a respectable one, and one could discuss it on its own merits. But, in this case, his book should bear the title, "The Fallacy of Development" instead of "Development Without Aid."

But if one accepts the validity of modern development, with all of its virtues and defects, the problem of foreign assistance of all kinds, from the point of view of the developing countries, is one or deciding the terms and conditions under which they want such assistance to come. It is up to them to decide which areas they will allow to be open to private foreign investors, for which areas they will seek to get assistance through intergovernmental or international channels, which sectors can be developed without any foreign help.

I would quarrel with one other detail of the Kohr model. This is his endorsement of what he calls "Development Communism." He makes a great distinction between it and what he calls "Ideological Communism," but it seems to me that this is largely a distinction without a difference. I agree with him that in today's world, a country which tries to develop completely by itself is almost certainly going to have to resort to the kind of tyranny which has been characteristic of Communism since at least the early days of the Stalin era. The only way you can get forced-draft industrialization in splendid isolation is by having a regime which kills or sends to concentration camps anyone who tries to object to the process of depriving workers and the rural population of all but the most rudimentary elements of food, clothing and shelter. But this is far from saying as he does that this is a good or desirable thing for any country to have to undergo. Quite to the contrary, it is exactly what it is most desirable to try to avoid. If by getting some help from outside, a country can avoid the burden of primitive living conditions and ferocious tyranny, it seems to me that this is all to the good.

There is only one thing certain about tyranny—and that is that there is tyranny. One has no way to be sure that the tyrant will be benificent. Nor is there any assurance, as Professor Kohr claims, that tyranny will pass when it has fulfilled what the Marxist-Leninist would call "its historic role." Tyrants have a way of liking to hang on to their jobs long after whatever little useful purpose they may have served has passed. It is therefore better, in my opinion, to avoid their coming to power in the first place.

Incidentally, as a kind of footnote, I would quarrel with the implication of Prof. Kohr's comparison of the Soviet's unaided development and the Jugoslav development-with-aid. The latter certainly has been infinitely more humane and civilized than was the terrorist experience of the Stalin regime in the U.S.S.R., and therefore much to be preferred.

When all of this is said, it seems to me that the great contribution of Dr. Kohr's book is that he emphasizes the value of paying more attention in the process of economic development to the possibilities of locally generated development on a municipal or regional scale, be it in arts and crafts, agriculture or simple types of industry. To too great a degree the attenion of economic development planners has been concentrated on large-scale projects involving large investments, and too little focus has undoubtedly been given to the possibilities of relatively small communities, through their own efforts and savings making significant contributions to national development and their own welfare. The community development programmes of a number of countries have been one attempt to enlist such local efforts. However, this has not been by any means sufficient. Dr. Kohr is undoubtedly correct when he argues that much more could be done by relatively small scale local efforts towards development than most developing countries have been able to achieve. However, I would argue that such efforts will in any case constitute a complement to the development programmes involving **modern** techniques, sizeable expenditures, and often foreign **exchange,** which in turn may involve "foreign aid" of one kind or **another.**

"You are happy, contented, and have no complaints."

Chapter Four

AUTHOR'S REPLY

*An important reason for their prosperity would seem
to have resulted from the nature of the country they
live in, since the sea that stretches beside it affords
no harbour; and so practically all the produce is
consumed by the natives.*
> —ATHENAEUS, ON THE INHABITANTS OF SYBARIS

IN the neighbourhood of my Austrian birthplace in the state of
Salzburg, hidden away in the silence of hills and forests, is a
brook feeding with its waters a series of three mills. Hence
the lovely melodious name *Dreimühlen*—Three Mills. I loved to
go there on hot summer afternoons as a schoolboy for strolls and
swims. Before returning, I invariably dropped into a little way-
side chapel that stood deserted and peaceful by the still waters of
the dammed up stream to look with fascination at one of those
charming primitive paintings depicting a drowning peasant youth
dressed in his Sunday best, a cross in his hands, his eyes prayer-
fully turned heavenwards, with only his chest and head still
out of the water. Underneath was the touching legend: "Here in
this quiet stream, driven by an irresistible urge to bathe though
he could not swim, perished Valentin Hennermann."

The picture so fascinated me that, when I returned to my village after an absence of 20 years, I again took a stroll through
the deep forest to Dreimühlen for a nostalgic reunion with the
old painting which I had so often cited for its charming legend.
It was still there at its old place, but to my surprise, I could not
see the central feature which had always attracted me as a boy
—the solemnly drowning figure of the peasant youth all prepared
to meet the Lord in his Sunday best. Finally I discovered it again,
but not where my vivid memory had placed it. Instead of occupying the centre of the picture, it turned out to be a very minor
feature in a corner, lost in the sweep of a wide panoramic view
of the landscape.

I was reminded of this when I read Professor R. J. Alexander's
comments on *Development Without Aid*. For I figured I had made

ample allowance for most of the things he criticizes, and given them a sufficiently featured position in my painting. But obviously, to many of my readers who, after all, are not the authors of what I have written, much of what I thought I had specially emphasized seems to have got as lost in an obscure corner of my tableau as the drowning boy was lost to me when I searched for him from a new perspective that could not see the detail for the whole. I am therefore grateful to my old friend for giving me the opportunity of restating a few of my positions to set not so much my record as the impression of my record straight.

1. Among others, Professor Alexander takes me to task for my advocacy, during a country's earliest development stages, of Development Communism for the purpose of avoiding Ideological Communism. He calls this a "distinction without a difference," and then proceeds to discredit the former by listing some of the outrages of the latter. If I were not familiar with the latter, I would have hardly had a reason for introducing the concept of the former. And if I introduced the former, I meant of course to create a distinction *with* a difference to show that, unlike ideological communism, development communism is by no means necessarily synonymous with the perpetration of outrages, nor tyranny for that matter with the deprivation of civic liberty. To that end I have listed on page 78 a number of historically unmonstrous forms of development communism such as "the Kibbutz communes of Israel, the monastic communes of the Catholic Church, the military communes of the Army, the sporting communes of rock climbers," etc. Having himself served as a soldier during World War II, I am sure Professor Alexander agrees with me that army communism and ideological communism is a distinction *with* a difference. And so is development communism which, unlike its ideological variant, is not the final but the militant phase of development. Similar to army communism, it is therefore doomed to fade in significance as victory approaches.

2. The same goes for its political concomitant: development authoritarianism, which is as different from its obnoxious variety as is development communism. This is why I listed as its representatives not Stalin or Castro whom Dr. Alexander had in mind, but Muñoz Marin or Peisistratus. For, as I specially stated on page 67, I used the term not in the modern but the ancient Greek

sense when the concept was "not yet besmirched by the degradation of later autocrats." Otherwise the wise Solon, who disliked *tyrannis,* could hardly have said that, were it not for this, he would consider Peisistratus the best of the Athenians. A further illustration making clear what I understood by development autocracy was my reference on page 108 to the historically highly successful and rarely abused "crisis" dictatorships of ancient Rome which proved that autocrats *will* adhere to constitutional limitations if societies have sufficiently advanced, particularly since the furtherance of advance is the chief reason for such temporary limitations. Moreover, to make doubly sure that my plea for both development communism and development autocracy would not be misunderstood, I stressed on page 70, that neither need extend into the realm of a citizen's non-economic concerns, as there is no reason why personal rights and freedom should not be safeguarded through institutions such as a Scandinavian type of Ombudsman.

This does not mean that I dispute Dr. Alexander's idea that tyrants like to hang on to power long after their usefulness has passed. But so of course do democrats. My main point was, that countries in the early stages of development do not have the choice between democracy and autocracy but, as Cyrus Sulzberger implied, between non-benevolent and benevolent despots; between ideological and development communism. And if I prefer the latter variey in both cases, it is not because I like them but, as I thought I had made clear on page 108, because "their success makes both dispensable." I agree, however, that perhaps in the larger context of my elaborations, my careful differentiation, which was illustrated by a number of historic examples, and seemed sharp enough to me as the author, became so lost to other readers that, like the drowning boy, it appeared as no more than a hazy "distinction without a difference" in an obscure corner of my tableau.

3. This probably explains also some of Professor Alexander's other criticisms, as when he suggests that I ignore that the world is no longer in the position it was in 1900. At that time, he concedes, my models might have been useful since many countries were still completely undeveloped. But since then, so much industrialization has been achieved even in them that any devel-

Development Without Aid

opment model failing to take this into account is an absurdity.

However, also in this case I *have* taken the alleged oversight into account by directing my proposals to those areas in undeveloped, underdeveloped, partially developed, and even developed countries which have remained untouched by the development of the past decades. I have therefore nowhere suggested the *tearing down* of Sao Paulo. What I have suggested is the *building up* of all those vast lands which, as in Brazil, have been left completely unaffected by their highly developed metropolitan regions. Because of the retardation of these vast lands, the Sao Paulos can obviously not live by them, nor they by their Sao Paulos. Why should they then continue to be linked in mutual trading ties that do not exist because the metropolis is more engrossed in its trading ties with more profitable developed foreign markets? For, as Myrdal showed by his theory of circular and cumulative causation, it is precisely because regions of unequal advance remain linked as single development units, that their relationship is not only completely sterile, advancing the advanced, and retarding the retarded; the sterility of the vast hinterlands is further increased by the depopulating Sao Paulo fixation of their inhabitants. This raises the question of how many of the 1,000,000 new jobs which Brazil must find each year are urban jobs becoming necessary not so much because of the population explosion, which I may ignore, as by rural depopulation which Professor Alexander ignores? Or how many of the "new" houses needed in Rio must be built not for those who have no houses but for those who have abandoned their houses in the countryside?

What I propose is therefore not, as Dr. Alexander suspects, a *return* to the *past* village state phase of an already overdeveloped Sao Paulo. It is the *creation* of *new* village states in the undeveloped immensity of the rest of the country by means of political subdivision. This will both put a stop to the unwholesome slumbreeding Sao Paulo fixation of the rural population, and insure that the new territorial entities will not again be sucked up by the self-centred gravitational fields of existing metropolitan sprawls whose attractive power has proved the chief cause that has kept the more distant reaches of the hinterlands in a state of such pre-medieval retardation that, by comparison, even the medieval village-state represents a significant advance. So if Professor Alexander agrees that my development models might be applicable to such completely undeveloped countries as Sikkim or Bhutan, he should have no objection to seeing them proposed for the thousands of even less developed Sikkims and Bhutans still stretching in 1972 across the vastnesses of Brazil, Ghana, or Bolivia as forlornly as they did in 1900. This does not *ignore* the already existing industries but proposes, exactly as he does, their complementation.

4. Moreover, my models should find an all the readier acceptance since they are backed by the theoretical speculations of some of the most outstanding economists of past and present, none of whom is known to have considered development a fallacy. There is for example Henry Charles Carey's *theory of molecular urban attraction* according to which the gravitational pull cities exert on their hinterland increases directly with their size and inversely with distance. As a result, the larger a city and the greater its distance-shrinking technological advance, the more will it deplete its rural environment of the human resources needed for its development. Another which I have repeatedly mentioned is Gunnar Myrdal's *theory of cumulative and circular causation,* according to which the market forces tying unequally developed areas together will, at a world level, tend "cumulatively to accentuate international inequalities" and, at a national level, "to increase, rather than to decrease, the inequalities between regions." There is Raul Prebisch's *law of increasing peripheral neglect* according to which the development needs of outlying regions are the more ignored the greater their distance from the centre. All these interpretations imply as the cause of economic retardation depletion of rural manpower resources, peripheral neglect, increasing polarization of inequalities. They do not attribute it to isolation of the more retarded regions but, on the contrary, to the ties that bind them to the more advanced—the rural regions to the cities, peripheral districts to the centre, underdeveloped areas to developed ones. But if ties are the cause of retardation, is it absurd to conclude that the cure might conceivably lie in the cutting of ties[1] rather than in the hopeless

1 To counter the centralizing and draining effect of a metropolis, Carey proposed the establishment of political autonomies in the form of rival cities that would contain the damaging attractive power of the central city. "The

strengthening of the hands trying to hold them at impossible odds in view of the giant forces pulling at them from the other end? And can someone suggesting, as I do from one end to the other, the *cutting* of ties, be accused of "ignoring the fact that they (the underdeveloped countries) are all more or less tied in with the rest of the world?"

5. My principal fault here was that it was I myself who put most of my witnesses, whom I should have featured in their Sunday best in the centre of my picture, into the obscure corners of footnotes in my reply to Professor Thorne. But even so, I could hardly have left any doubt that what I advocated in no uncertain terms in *Development Without Aid* for both undeveloped and underdeveloped countries is not, as Professor Alexander suggests, the *Fallacy of Development,* but the *Fallacy of Inappropriate Development.* As I emphasized throughout my book up to its summation in the postscript on page 118: all my models are designed to foster advance! "But it is measured advance; unaided advance; *appropriate* advance." This does not mean a return to the village state. It suggests the village state where there is as yet nothing; the inward-looking city state where there exists already the strong elemental nucleus of prosperous rural communities; the introduction of small-scale manufacturing—E. F. Schumacher's famous "intermediate technology"—where economic integration is as yet confined to small areas; and of larger industries where markets have become wider as the result of the fusion of already advanced regional economies. In other words, I offer the shoe that fits the actual, not the desired, stage of growth: to a baby a baby's shoe, not a grown-up's; to an adolescent an adolescent's, not a baby's. Does this imply that I consider growth a fallacy?

What seems fallacious is the analogy by which Professor Alexander rejects as "natural" my historic order of phases through which all nations must pass if their development is to be healthy. He says rightly that a modern soldier no longer needs to run

centralizing tendency of the State Capital is, in its turn, greatly neutralized by the existence of opposing centres of attraction at the various county seats, and in the numerous towns and cities of the Union, each managing its own affairs . . ." H. C. Carey, *Principles of Social Science,* Philadelphia: J. B. Lippincott, 1858, p. 44.

through a slingshot and bow-and-arrow phase. But the reason for this is not, as he suggests, that the twentieth century has outgrown that stage by 400 years, but that a draftee in his early twenties has outgrown it by at least 10. Having outgrown it, does however not mean that he did not have to pass through the pre-military slingshot phase himself as a boy on his way to becoming a good soldier. For no accumulation of historic *social* experience relieves the individual of the necessity of *personally* experiencing all the phases of the maturing process again and again. Even a genius starts his terrestrial journey as a child, laboriously picking out words and grammar, and practicing with primeval slingshot shouts before he is able to assemble them in the form of polished modern machine-gun orations.

If Dr. Alexander straightens out his analogy, it will put also another of my main points in its proper light: the brevity of time needed for passing through the socio-biologically necessary phases of healthy growth. This is the very opposite of what he ascribes to me when he suspects me of suggesting that the presently developing nations "should be required to go through four centuries themselves before they can be highly developed." For I have emphasized again and again as one of my principal arguments, amply backed by historic examples, the tremendous speed with which unaided development can be achieved from the most primitive beginnings to the most sophisticated culmination, provided that none of the essential steps is skipped. In each case, I underlined the time involved was not of many centuries, nor even one, but a single generation, as when I quoted Pausanias on Peisistratus (p. 62), or Augustus on himself (p. 62)—"I found Rome brick and leave it marble." And what about my reference to Mr. Hlady of the Canadian Indian Service (p. 63) who developed a community at the cost of $12.64 in six months?

6. Finally, Professor Alexander takes me to task for misreading American history when I use the United States as an example for unaided development. I do not think I misread the American experience of the 19th Century. Nor do I suggest that Professor Alexander is wrong when he stresses the important contribution rendered to American development by foreign investment. We are simply impressed by different stages of American development. Foreign investment and trade have of course played a

role. After all, there was a time when all Americans were foreigners. When they opened up the country, they established a government of foreigners, by foreigners, for foreigners. And the foreign-oriented agricultural and trading pattern prevailed even after independence.

This cast, indeed, the early United States into a different mould from that which determined the economies of the more self-sufficiently developed inner directed European countries. But after it had performed its great initial function of opening up an as yet empty continent in its vague outlines, America's foreign-oriented market, trading, and investment pattern was considered by contemporary opinion no longer a blessing fostering progress but a curse nurturing distortion, imbalance, economic depend-ence, retardation, and exploitation. This is why Charles Henry Carey, the greatest of her early economists, advocated for the partially developed United States of *his* time very much what I advocate for countries finding themselves in the same position in *ours*. That is to say, he did not propose the undoing of what had already been done (as I do not propose it either), but the build-up of the undone part of the American economy along radi-cally different lines: away from its expensive foreign-investment backed, lopsided market dependence in the direction of cost-saving self-sufficiency. Making a distinction (without a differ-ence?) between *commerce* (interchange within a community), which he hailed, and *trade* (inter-change between communities), which he condemned on the ground that the latter's far-flung transportation is "the first and heaviest tax to be paid by land and labour,"[1] he demanded, unlike his contemporary counter-parts, not foreign assistance but protective isolation from exter-nal involvements. And instead of savings of scale resulting from regional specialization, he offered as his development target the concentrated establishment of all complementary economic activities within the narrow geographic confines of what I have

---

[1] "The first and heaviest tax to be paid on land and labour is transporta-tion . . . It increases in geometrical proportion, as the distance from the market increases arithmetically." H. C. Carey, *op. cit.*, p. 271. In another pas-sage he writes that transportation "seeks to augment the difficulties lying between the consumer and the producer, while building up the fortune of those who stand between them." Ibid. p. 438.

called the village state, causing "the loom and the anvil to take their natural places by the side of the plough and the harrow."

Now, if I read American history correctly, what Henry Charles Carey—whom Sir Alexander Gray calls "the supreme example of the truth that the economist reflects his environment"—rationalized was exactly what happened.. This does not make Professor Alexander wrong in portraying America's foreign involvement that came before and to a lesser extent after. But neither does Professor Alexander make *my* picture wrong which aimed at describing what came in between. And it is this in-between phase—the heroic phase of American development—which, correcting the distortions of the first, and preparing the ground for the outwardly more dramatic third phase, not only conforms to my model but also contributed the main features of the American identity. And, if we can trust the testimony of the nationalist school of American economic thought, the lasting nature of the subsequent success of this phase was due to the fact that it did precisely what the more advanced great English economists of the time said was fallacious and could not be done: it made up for partially skipping the pre-trading self-sufficiency and independence strengthening phase by taking not one but two steps back. In vast areas it "regressed" even beyond the village state into the still earlier phase of the isolated farm state (whose vigour in the dim European Middle Ages left such an imprint that it is still discernible in places such as Tyrol, Switzerland, or Devon).[1]

The self-sufficiency that now underpinned the previously un-balanced, lopsided, foreign-investment financed colonial-type but, henceforth, proportionally considerably less important trade structure of the United States produced of course quite a different picture from what we would nowadays understand by a progressive economy. It became eminently rural and innerdirected even in its industrialization but certainly not less enriching. Able to do without an excessive amount of transport and marketing capital, it saved in the means. But this did not signify that it was on that ground deficient in attaining what was more important:

[1] For example see W. G. Hoskins, *Devon farms without a village*, in *The Listener*, July 15, 1965.

the end. On the contrary! Since the means of far-flung internationally integrated development such as road networks, high-speed vehicles, large-scale modern industry, etc., are, as Dr. Alexander himself admits, "usually exactly the things for which it is necessary to obtain foreign exchange," a country changing in the terms of Carey from "trade" back to "commerce" can not only develop rapidly without the undignified dependence on that foreign exchange but, as I have tried to establish, reach levels of advance which, though of a radically different nature from those achieved with the help of a capital devouring machine civilization of the modern type, can hardly be considered inferior.

7. To get a dramatic picture of the prosperity attainable in regional tradeless though not commerceless isolation we need, however, not go back to the flourishing farm and village-state settlements of 19th-Century America. There are splendid examples of such communities thriving in the midst of the otherwise highly integrated United States of our own time. As in the case of their ancestors, theirs is to this day an affluence of self-sufficiency. For it is self-sufficiency that relieves them of the burden of maintaining the shiny armour of streamlined transport equipment which the economic establishment considers social wealth, while to anyone with horsesense it is but "the first and heaviest cost to be paid by man and labour," its abundance measuring not the high standard but the high cost of life.

My reference is to the numerous Amish and Mennonite communities. In the words of Charles Wheeler (*The Listener,* August 5, 1965), they continue even today to "shun the motor car, preferring the horse and buggy, and avoid electricity like the plague—partly because it would make them dependent, but also because it would bring into the home harmful influences, like radio, television, and the telephone." They run their own schools, "firmly taking their children out of the classroom at fifteen, and they look after their own aged and poor." Yet, using old-fashioned ploughs instead of tractors, and handfashioned tools of such functional elegance that they have become exhibition pieces in museums of modern art, of all places, they are not only free of unemployment (and consequently also of juvenile delinquency) problems; their houses are the most sturdy, their furniture the most solid, their environments the most neat, their standards the most set, their cattle the most nourished, and their fields amongst the best tended and highest in yield in the world, outdistancing in this respect even the most mechanized farms around them. And while the rest of the interdependent, aid-giving, affluent United States has its hands full with a war on the shocking proportions of its own poverty, the inward looking enclaves of Mennonites and Amish are so contemptuous of the very idea of outside aid that "recently Congress, following the example of the local authorities, approved a bill giving the Amish exemption from paying social security taxes."

Charles Rice and Rolling Steinmetz have well explained how such high prosperity could be achieved with so little in modern equipment. While the plough of Amish farmer Elam Stolzfus "was shearing through the damp brown loam on hilltop and lowland alike, the non-Amish farmer next door wasn't ploughing at all. His pretty red tractor stood idle in the barn, for the tractor was too heavy for the soil of this warm and windy March morning."[1] And, of course, in contrast to the ox, the tractor feeding on gasoline returns nothing to the earth to make it more fertile, cannot reach edges, ridges, or corners accessible to the plough, and is likely to damage the delicate limestone structure of the sub-soil.[2] Also in mechanical respects, the dexterity of the Amish is such that "long before Detroit began manufacturing automobiles with three distinct body styles, the Amish carriage maker was turning out the buggy equivalent of the convertible, the sedan and the stationwagon."[3] Is it really such an absurdity to suggest to impecunious underdeveloped countries to engage Amish and Mennonite consultants to teach them how to produce, rather than

[1] Charles S. Rice and Rolling C. Steinmetz. *The Amish Year*. Rutgers University Press, 1956, p. 62.

[2] As Vincent R. Tortora writes in *The Amish Folk* (Lancaster: Photo Arts Press, 1962, p. 7), many agricultural experts seem therefore rightly to "contend the Amish reluctance to accept motorized tractors has contributed greatly to their increased yields. For one, they can get ploughs into their muddy fields earlier in the spring with horses or mules than they could with tractors. Secondly, animals are much lighter than tractors and are less likely to break down the delicate sub-soil limestone structure.—The more earthly Amish farmer puts his preference for animals thusly: 'Well, if you put gasoline in a tractor, all you get is smoke'."

[3] Ibid., p. 7.

Harvard and MIT missionaries to teach them how to trade, integrate, make friends in Washington, and influence foreign investors?

8. This does not necessarily mean that I advocate the Amish way of life. I don't. What I do is: advocate it as a *first step* after which other aspirations may bring in other systems. Hence there is no reason why its advocacy for countries whose rural regions degenerate because of their obsession with an urbanized car and television industrialization, should be considered as a plea for arresting the development of peoples whose deficiency lies not in car jams or television sets but in food, shelter, and clothing, the very things in the production of which the Mennonite and Amish ways excel, while the international way of intertwined trading and assistance so obviously does not. For why should there otherwise be such need for help?

Nor do I see why the sacred cows of prematurely constructed, trade-feeding industries should be an obstacle to belatedly building up the untended pastures of lopsidedly developed countries by replacing their excessive world-oriented "intertie" structure with a system of capital-saving, labour-using, and hence full-employment=ensuring isolated village states after the Mennonite and Amish pattern. This may sound regressive. But even if one ignores all other advantages, will not the small self-sufficient village state have the same function in the age of the impending atomic catastrophe which the Ark of Noah had in the age of the Great Deluge, when survival depended likewise not on a mutual-help "intertie" structure but, on the contrary, on separation from it?

If this is not realized soon, what will happen when the first bomb drops on the nerve centres of a senselessly hooked-up homogenized civilization is what happened to the highly integrated North East region of North America on November 9, 1965, when part of its electric power gave out. Instead of a compensatory light stream racing from the huge unaffected area to help the small affected region, a reverse chain reaction produced by the vaunted "intertie" power system spread inkspsot darkness from the small affected area over the huge unaffected one. Would Professor Alexander call the subsequent reaction of the Canadian Government to cut itself loose from an otherwise profitable

"intertie" regressive? Or share the antediluvian experts' conviction that Noah's Ark was an absurdity? According to the Bible,
it was the absurd who survived the Deluge, not the experts, as it
will be the Amish village states that will form the cells of new
life after the atomic catastrophe, not the automated nation states.
With André Gide, another dispenser of absurdities, "I believe in
the virtue of small nations. I believe in the virtue of small numbers. The world will be saved by the few."

9. In conclusion, I should like to come back to what I said at
the beginning. I composed a picture of which, in my capacity as
its author, I know where I placed the details. But this does not
necessarily mean that other readers can spot in them the significance I meant to assign to some of them. If I am wrongly interpreted, or suspected of creating distinctions without a seeming
difference, I readily agree that the fault may be mine rather than
Professor Alexander's. My only excuse is that I meant to write a
short book, not a long one, and thus had to sacrifice amplifica-
tions that might have made my intentions clearer. But I would
have been misinterpreted anyway, as anyone always will who
advances something outside the stream of established thought.

It is particularly because of this that I am grateful to my old
friend for affording me by his sharp criticism the opportunity of
clarifying what I have said not by correcting but by repeating
it; and adding a few examples such as the extraordinary welfare
record of the Mennonite and Amish experience which I failed
to include in my original text. Moreover, I feel that our positions
are not really so different as the dialogue seems to imply. Dr.
Alexander agrees with me that local and regional effort should be
given greater prominence in national and international program-
ming, which, after all, was my main point; and *I* concede that the
two should be complementary.

It is only in the question of what should complement what
that our positions remain radically different. Professor Alexander
thinks the regional scale should complement the world scale. *I:*
the world's the region's. He thinks the plough should complement
the tractor. *I:* the tractor the plough. For as long as countries
are underdeveloped, the experience of history seems to indicate
that the plough is a superior tool to the tractor not only for laying a healthy foundation for later mechanized economic develop-

ment but, what is nowadays of even greater importance in the eyes of nation builders, for the creation of a strong national identity.[1] This is why the Puerto Rican nationalists have unwittingly chosen as their slogan *Jibaro Si—Yankee No,* rather than *Mecanico Si* which would fundamentally mean the same as *Yankee Si.*

THE FRUIT OF MENNONITE INTERMEDIATE TECHNOLOGY: HIGH QUALITY, FULL EMPLOYMENT, SELF-SUFFICENCY.

[1] I have developed this point more extensively in a chapter in *The Overdeveloped Nations* entitled *Economic Development versus National Identity* (Dusseldorf: Econ-Verlag, 1962; Barcelona: Editorial Luis Miracle, 1965). But lest my reference to the "plough" be taken too narrowly, I want to stress that it should be understood in the more functional sense of D. E. F. Schumacher's "intermediate" rather than primitive technology.

Chapter Five

A FINAL COMMENT

By Professor Alfred Thorne

All's well that ends well.
—SHAKESPEARE

VARIETY is the spice of life; not merely also, but more so, in academe. Professor Kohr's imaginative views undoubtedly diversify and enrich our intellectual diet, with this book, as with previous ones.

One Sunday morning, some years ago, a charming senior member of the British Guiana, now Guyana, civil service came to my home here in Puerto Rico to enquire, on behalf of the colony's political chief, whether I would return to be special economic adviser to the chief. Having observed how, in underdeveloped countries generally, soft loans or aid could be obtained with much less difficulty for some purposes, for example house-building, than for others more fundamentally related to true development, such as establishing technical schools and manufacturing enterprises, I offered my guest some free advice for his chief—while I introduced to the obviously well-educated palate of my scholarly fellow West Indian a few of the famous brands of Puerto Rico's rum.

Among the main items of advice were that, first, the colony should be wary of soliciting or accepting soft loans for programmes or projects that did not fit in with its own logical priorities for development; and second, that it should refuse soft loans that would add more to the colony's future liabilities for interest and debt repayment than they would add to the colony's capacity to produce sufficient new income out of which to repay the debt and meet the service charges. Better no aid than bad aid, I cautioned. Fresh in my mind were the tragic economic experiences of a few countries I had recently visited. A large part of Professor Kohr's main thrust, therefore, has appealed strongly to me from the outset.

But I also still hold that appropriate or good use of soft loans, together with the usually prescribed domestic efforts, such as saving, makes the development process less burdensome and more efficient. Perhaps the real difference remaining between Professor Kohr and myself on this is that I am still optimistic, and have not abandoned hope that the advanced countries are capable of some genuine decency, after all. Some events subsequent to the writing of my earlier comments seem to confirm my optimism, now admittedly less sparkling though, that soft loans can be helpful when applied appropriately, not to distort priorities and technologies.

Nor do I abandon my conviction, based on the established, unshaken, historical record, that the descendants of the exploited colonial peoples have as much moral right to some share in the now enlarged modern economic pie as the descendants of the old exploited metropolitan working class populations have. The philosophy of the Welfare State now justifies this increased sharing by the present-day working class, and even middle-class, descendants of the formerly exploited working class of the rich countries. But it required much persistence and stubborn pressures on the part of the leaders of the rich countries' lower classes over decades, to gain finally enlarged shares. It is only comparatively recently that changes in the international distribution of political power and other transformations have favoured and stimulated the rise of corresponding pressures from the leaders of the descendants of the colonial exploited.

Just as the accumulation of the first five thousand dollars of capital was, and still is, more difficult for poor families than adding the second or third five thousand, so also the accumulation of the first millions of industrial capital was much more painful than the present annual additions of billions of capital in the now rich countries. Gross underpayment of the ancestors of the working and middle classes of the now rich countries, in the days before trade unions became legal and before there were minimum wage laws, constituted forced saving and forced contribution to the formation of the first basic industrial capital of those countries. Their descendants are now recipients in one way or another, in the welfare states, of the dividends accruing from the forced investments of their ancestors. In the underdeveloped countries, it was not a question of underpayment only, or principally, but of non-payment. The descendants of the working classes in both rich and poor countries are demanding their moral inheritance. Yet, it is important, extremely so, that they do not accept it in forms, or with strings attached, that would hurt them in the long run not only economically but otherwise.

Yet, I do not claim that the present wealth of the rich countries is due only to their exploitation of their own working classes and the colonial ones. It would be as immoral for me to deny the enormous contributions of the early entrepreneurs and thinkers of the now rich countries, as it would be for persons in rich countries—and few do—to deny the enormous recorded, crucially important, early contributions of the colonial and plantation workers.

For more than a decade, now, several poor countries have been trying to correct the severe distortions in their economies and their patterns of external trade, both legacies of colonialism. Some have succeeded significantly in reducing their dependence on imported foods, clothing and other consumer goods, and in expanding the range of their exports from two or three unprocessed agricultural or mineral products to several dozens of important items, including some articles of light manufacture. In several cases, however, the rich countries have raised barriers to these embryonic competitors. Sometimes the barrier is unpublicised. For example, I shall never forget the embarrassment of the United States Ambassador to Jamaica on the occasion when, early in 1964, he had to brief us, members of a visiting United States AID mission, that he had just received instructions from Washington that he must require the Government of that island to reduce its exports of certain light manufactures to rich America!

Asking for fair trade is not asking a favour. It is merely seeking to get some of the rich signatories of international trade and tariff agreements to honour their signatures and abandon unfair trade practices.

Incidentally, the phrase "favourable trend in the terms of trade" has nothing to do with any favour being sought or granted. It is only a trend in the relationship between average price of a country's exports and average price of its imports. The trend is favourable when it reflects that the prices of the country's exports are rising more quickly (or falling more slowly) than the prices of its imports. Countries that export unprocessed products, that is, poorer countries, have usually experienced unfavourable terms of trade trends over the long haul—even after allowing for quality improvements in the manufactures they import.

Should Hong Kong's four million hardworking citizens stop exporting its main products—clothing and a variety of other light manufactures—and, instead, try to produce all the food they require on the paltry 380 square miles of land they have? Would this be a better path towards development than the one they have been brilliantly pursuing with such great success these three decades? Hardly. Neither should small Puerto Rico, Jamaica, Barbados, Costa Rica and dozens of other poor countries abandon their efforts to diversify their trade and thereby to sell what brings them better relative prices, and higher levels of living.

Recommending that these countries withdraw from all external trade and try to be self-sufficient seems much like suggesting that a poor, semi-literate farm family should confine all the energies of its members to satisfying directly one another's needs, from within its one-acre family plot, rather than have one member sell some of his labour services to a larger farmer, another sell his skill as a haircutter to neighbours, and so on, and use the proceeds of these sales to buy an occasional piece of codfish or a bit of medical advice for the family—which it cannot supply to itself. Several of the poor countries are merely exercising their recently acquired rights and options to choose their own special trading partners, with whom to share the gains from trade, and to determine the patterns of that trade to suit themselves.

But Professor Kohr is, again, undoubtedly right to warn the little lambs to beware of getting close to the huge wolves. I would say: trade with the giants, but warily and selectively; if this is not possible, then take *part* of Professor Kohr's advice and avoid all

A Final Comment

trade with the giants. And take *all* of Professor Kohr's advice in regard to size. Choose quality of life over quantity of hardware.

Drawing by Alan Dunn ©
The New Yorker Magazine, Inc.

"It's good to get home!"

BIBLIOGRAPHY

BOOKS CITED[1]

Aquinas, St. Thomas, *Government of Rulers*, 141

Aristotle, *Politics*, 46n.

Augustine, St., *The City of God*, 160, 165n.

Bach, Kurt, *Slums, Projects and People*, 112.

Baransky, N. N., *Economic Geography of the Soviet Union*, 145n.

Blum, F. H., *Work and Community —the Scott-Bader Commonwealth and the Quest for a New Order*, 44n.

Cambridge University, *Cambridge History of the British Empire*, 128.

Carcopino, Jerome, *Daily Life in Ancient Rome*, 138n.

Carey, Henry Charles, *Principles of Social Science*, 37n.
— *Harmony of Interests*, 38n.

Chardon, Carlos E., *Datos que Sugieren la Integracion de Una Parte de la Region del Caribe: La Republica Dominicana y Puerto Rico*, 142

Cunningham, W., *The Growth of English Industry and Commerce*, 129n.

Dasgupta, Sugata, *A Great Society of Small Communities*, 44n.

Evans, Gwynfor, *Wales and the Common Market*, 143

Gee, J., *The Trade and Navigation of Great Britain considered*, 127

Gibbon, Edward, *Decline and Fall of the Roman Empire*, 172n.

Goetz, Kurt, Dr. Med. *Hiob Praetorius*, 154

Gray, Sir Alexander, *The Development of Economic Doctrine*, 37n., 147n.

Henderson, O., *The Zollverein*, 35n., 144

Hlady, Walter M., *A Community Development Project Amongst The Churchill Band at Churchill, Manitoba*, 63n.

Hobsbawm, E. J., *Industry and Empire*, 167n.

Horace, *Carmina*, 166

Hornick, Philip von, *Oesterreich Ueber Alles Wenn Es Nur Will*, 147

Keynes, Maynard, *Plan for an International Clearing Union*, 43n.

Kohr, Leopold, *The Breakdown of Nations*, 41n.
— *Customs Unions — A Tool Of Peace*, 43n.
— *El Superdesarrollo — El peligro del Gigantismo*, 117n.
— *Weniger Staat (Freedom from Government)*, 111n.

Kumar, Satish, *Non-Violence or Non-Existence*, 44n.

Lichtheim, George, *Imperialism*, 167n.

Lord, J., *Capital and Steam Power*, 128

Mackintosh, J. P., *Devolution of Power*, 45n.

Marx, Karl, *Communist Manifesto*, 61

Montchrétien, Antoine de, *Traicté de l'OEconomie Politique*, 147.

Myrdal, Gunnar, *Rich Lands and Poor*, 22n.

Owen, Robert, *Report to the County of Lanark*, 44

Plutarch, *Life of Lycurgus*, 59

Puerto Rican Planning Board, *Ingreso y Producto*, 151n.

---

[1] Full publication references are found on the pages listed with titles.

Rees, J. F., *The Phase of British Commercial Policy in the 18th Century*, 127n.
Rice, Charles S., and Steinmetz, Rolling C., *The Amish Year*, 191n.
Robinson, Austin, *The Economic Consequences of the Size of Nations*, 42n., 158n.

Seers, Dudley, *A Model of Comparative Rates of Growth*, 130n.
Simons, Henry, *Economic Policy for a Free Society*, 170
Singer, Hans, *International Development—Growth and Change*, 43n.
Smith, Adam, *Wealth of Nations*, 93, 126, 126n.
Smith, Raymond T., *British Guiana*, 129n.
Steuart, Sir James, *Principles of Political Economy*, 93
Strachey, John, *The Great Awakening*, 159
Stubbs, Joyce, *Greek Cookery*, 23n.
Suetonius, *Life of Vespasian*, 117n.

Temporary National Economic Committe, *Relative Efficiency of Large, Medium-sized, and Small Business*, 96n.
Tortora, Vincent R., *The Amish Folk*, 191n.
Toynbe, Arnold J., *A Study of History*, 147n.

United Nations, *Report of the Economic Commission for Latin America*, 133.

Villari, Pasquale, *Life and Times of Savonarola*, 162n.
Viner, Jacob, *The Customs Union Issue*, 142

Williams, Eric, *Capitalism and Slavery*, 127n.
Wood, William, *A Survey of Trade*, 127

Young, Arthur, *Travels in France and Italy*, 31n.

ARTICLES CITED

Balogh, Thomas, "Notes on the U.N. Conference on Trade and Development", *Bulletin of Economics and Statistics*, 131n.
Bhave, Vinoba, "Atomic Age Independence", *Resurgence*, Vol. 1, No. 12; 44n.
Brook, Paul, "The Golden Plains of Tanganyika", *Horizon*, Vol. VIII, No. 1; 96n.

Gillman, Joseph M., "Ricardo's Development as an Economist", *Science and Society*, Vol. XX, No. 3. 173.

Hoskins, W. C., "Devon Farms Without a Village", *The Listener*, July 15, 1965, 189n.
Huxley, Julian, "Biological Improvement", *The Listener*, November 1, 1951; 95n.

Kohr, Leopold, "The Aspirin Standard", *Business Quarterly*, Summer 1956; 41n.
— "The History of the Common Market", *Journal of Economic History*, September 1960; 143n.
— "Toward a New Measurement of Living Standards", *The American Journal of Economics and Sociology*. October 1955; 41n.
— "Velocity Theory of Population", *Land Economics*. May 1958, Vol. XXXIV, No. 2; 54n.

Robinson, Joan, "Chinese Communes", *The Listener*, January 30, 1964; 79n.-80n, 81n, 111n.

Schumacher, E. F., "Buddhist Economics", *Resurgence*, Vol. 1, No. 11; 43n.
— "Industrialization through Intermediate Technology", *Resurgence*, Vol 1, No. 2; 43n.
— "Industrial Society", *Resurgence*, Vol. 1, No. 3; 43n.
— "Multilateral Clearing", *Economica*, Spring 1943; 43n.
— "The New Economics", *Resurgence*, Vol. 2, No. 3; 43n.
Sen, A. C., "Gramdan", *Resurgence*, Vol. 2, Nos. 8/9; 44n.

NEWSPAPERS AND PERIODICALS CITED

INDEX OF NAMES

INDEX OF PLACES

INDEX OF SUBJECTS

Index

Index

Index

Speed of unassisted economic growth, 13, 62-65, 176, 187

Sputnik, opiate of, 68

Squandermania, of native leaders, 33, 33n.; 74; of author, 74n.-75n.

Square, meaning of, in pattern of city, 47; aesthetic aspects of, 48; proper components of, 49; of chess board, story of invention of game, 52

State intervention, causes of, 109

Statistics: populations of small communities, 19; variability of menu of country inn, 23; living standards in U.S., U.S.S.R., and Loiza Aldea, 26-27; squandermania in Dahomey, 33n.; 74; Swiss economy, 41; national and personal consumption, 41n.; diseconomies of scale, 50n.-51n., 101n.; rising traffic complexities, 52, 54; postwar production programmes, 60; development of Manitoba Indians, 63, 63n.; efficiency of small scale in U.S.S.R., 80n.; in Vietnam, 93; housing deficiency in Latin America, 81n.-82n.; economic division of U.S.S.R., 98n.; and of Common Market, 99n.; wage rules in Brasil and New York World Fair, 112n.-113n.; widening gap of inequality in Puerto Rico, 116n.; profits from colonies, 124, 126, 127; Russian aid to Cuba, 133; numbers of women to men, 140; Puerto Rico's import dependence, 151n.; destitution in England, 159, 164n.

Status symbol: living at working place, 48

Steel mills, new objects of tribal worship, 21, 168; Ceylon in search of, 152

Subsistence, base, narrowed by integration, 96n.; — farmer, location of, in early U.S., 175; — level, raising the individual above, 79, 166, 170

Suburbanization, caused by motorized existence, 32; cost of, 52; cancer of, 85

Sugar planters, treatment of, 130

Summum bonum, by self-sufficiency, 24; components of, 31, (the good life), 40, 104

Surplus, graduates, 70; — labour, released by culminated village-state, 85; — product, taking form of urban, military, and imperial capital, 162-163

Surplus value, agents withholding it: private entrepreneur, 67; communism, 68; more withheld from domestic than colonial labour, 156, 157; needed for financing vast scale of state, 160-161, 161n.; partial release of, to workers by welfare state, 165; further release of, through dismemberment of large political units, 165

Symposium, Greek meaning of, 122

Tabula rasa, of ancient Jews, 109

Teamster Union, not welfare but power complex, 101; wage rates of, 113n.

Tower of Babel, monopolistic unistructure of, 91n.

Tractor, limited suitability of, 191, 191n., 193

Trade, as mechanism of stagnation between regions of unequal advance, 22n.; wastes of, 84; interregional limitation of, 99; losses through colonial terms of, 124, 125; 136-139, 136n.; imperial profits of, 126; century of, 127; slave —, as foundation of all the rest, 127; distortion of colonial economies by, 128-130, 197; Golden Age of Greece founded on, 130; intellectual stimulus of, 131; intercolonial prohibitions of, 131; unwisdom of development of, by and for —, 137-141, 152; favourable terms as result not of concession, but of power to, 137; distortion through aid, 139; as basis of dependence, 140; reasons for successful — in *Zollverein*, 144; conditions for profitable —, 146; first glory of Greece not founded on, 148; absurdity of reduction of, 153, 184-185, 186; method of improving terms of, 171, 198; U.S. historic involvement in, 175, 188; Carey's distinction between commerce and —, 188, 190; unhelpfulness of, in raising living standards, 192; beware of giants as partners in, 198

Traffic, aggravation of, by improvement, 53-54; per-capita increase

ILLUSTRATIONS